# Early Farmers of West Mediterranean Europe

Archaeology editor

**Dr John Coles**
University of Cambridge

# Early Farmers of West Mediterranean Europe

## Patricia Phillips

Lecturer in Prehistory and Archaeology
University of Sheffield

Hutchinson of London

Hutchinson & Co (Publishers) Ltd
3 Fitzroy Square, London W1

London Melbourne Sydney Auckland
Wellington Johannesburg and agencies
throughout the world

First published 1975
© Patricia Phillips 1975

Illustrations © Hutchinson & Co (Publishers) Ltd 1975

Set in Monotype Times
Printed in Great Britain by The Anchor Press Ltd
and bound by Wm Brendon & Son Ltd
both of Tiptree, Essex

ISBN 0 09 123971 0

# Contents

*To my mother and father*

# Acknowledgements

The idea for this book originated with the author's thesis work for the University of London Institute of Archaeology, but the majority of the writing and much further research took place during the tenure of a Research Fellowship and later Lectureship in the Department of Ancient History, University of Sheffield. The author is grateful for research awards received from the University of London Research Fund and the University of Sheffield Research Fund.

The author would like to thank Professor R. J. Hopper, of the Department of Ancient History, University of Sheffield, and her five colleagues teaching Prehistory and Archaeology in the same Department, for their advice and encouragement during the writing of this book. Any and all faults, however, are the author's sole responsibility. Two secretaries of the Ancient History Department, Mrs Dorothy Cruse and Mrs Jean Hampshire, typed and re-typed the manuscript most patiently. Miss Susan Bird NDD, of Cley-next-the-Sea, Norfolk, drew all the illustrations after originals supplied by the author. Plates 2 and 7 were printed by the Geography Department of Sheffield University and Plates 1 and 8 by Michael Harvey AIIP of the University of Sheffield Television Service, from the author's negatives.

Innumerable archaeologists and museum curators have helped to provide material and ideas which have gone into this book, notably Dr Jean Courtin of Marseille, with whom the author has spent many interesting hours of excavation and discussion. Grateful thanks are also due to Messrs J. Arnal, G. Costantini, M. Escalon de Fonton, S. Gagnière, J. Guilaine, R. Jeantet, R. Montjardin and J. L. Roudil in France; Messrs Grosjean and Lanfranchi in Corsica; Professor Contu and Dttssa Lo Schiavo in Sardinia; Professor Muñoz and Dr Fletcher Vals in Spain; and Dr Guerreschi and Professor Radmilli in Italy. In England Dr Barfield and Dr Trump gave helpful advice about the Italian and Sardinian Neolithic.

The author is particularly indebted to the curators of the following museums for the possibility of studying collections over a long period. At Nîmes Museum of Natural History it was possible to draw material from the Neolithic of the surrounding area (Figures 5, 8, 20) and obtain photographs of local statue-menhirs (Plate 5). Figures 6 and 17 were drawn from original sherds in the Montserrat Monastery Museum (Figures 6:1, 2 and Figures 17:8–10), the Barcelona Historical Museum (Figure 6:4) and the Museum of Moya (Figure 6:3 and Figure 17:1–7). Figure 22 was drawn from material stored in the Musée Réattu, Arles, Figure 9:3 from an original in the Museo di Archeologia Ligure, Genoa, and Figure 9:1–3 from originals in the St-Rémy-de-Provence Museum (Bouches-du-Rhône). The Sardinian sequence was studied in the Sassari Museum.

For other figures the author has re-drawn originals from the following publications

Figure 1 – Leale Anfassi, 1972, fig. 29
Figure 2 – Bailloud, 1969, figs. 25; 20.1; 19.3, 9; 24; 18.1
　　　　　 Lanfranchi and Weiss, 1972, figs. 5.3, 6.1
　　　　　 Lanfranchi, 1973, fig. 23
　　　　　 Atzeni, 1966, plate 7.20, 9, 13
Figure 3 – Photograph from Museo di Archeologia Ligure, Genoa,
　　　　　 Guilaine and Muñoz; 1964, fig. 2
　　　　　 Montjardin, private photograph
Figure 4 – Manfredini, 1972, figs. 4, 7, 39
Figure 7 – Malavolti, 1953, plates 6.1, 4; plates 5, 22
　　　　　 Bagolini and De Marinis, 1973, figs. 3, 5
Figure 9 – No. 4, after Castelfranco, 1913, plate XIV.18
　　　　　 No. 5, Guerreschi, 1967, fig. 327
Figure 10 – Courtin and Pélouard, 1971, fig. 3
Figure 13 – Méroc and Simonnet, 1969, p. 29
Figure 14 – Nos. 1, 2, Bailloud, 1969, fig. 12.2, 3
Figure 15 – Puxeddu, 1955–7
Figure 16 – No. 1, Bailloud, 1969, fig. 10.19
　　　　　　No. 2, Courtin, 1970, fig, 5.6
　　　　　　No. 3, Ripoll and Llongueras, 1967, fig. 5
Figure 18 – Guerreschi, 1969, figs. 32, 33, 162, 113, 139, 185, 256, 308, 299, 328
Figure 19 – Gagnière and Granier, 1963, figs. 20, 8, 23–4, 4, 3
Figure 21 – Salles, 1970, fig. 1; fig. 4.1, 18, 20, 19, 21, 22, 26, 5; fig. 3.8
Figure 23 – Drawing by Bailloud *in* Escalon de Fonton, 1966, fig. 28

Figure 24 – Roudil, 1966, figs. 5, 9
Figure 25 – Leisner and Leisner, 1943, fig. 9.1; 1.1, 14, 23, 18, 24, 25, 33 and plates 20.2; 2.4, 7
Figure 26 – Contu, 1964, plates 4, 5

Plate 7 illustrates the stone-walled house of the Fontbouïsse culture presently under excavation at Cambous (Hérault) by Fr Canet; the author is grateful to Fr Canet and J. L. Roudil for permitting the publication of this photograph.

*Sheffield, June 1974*

# List of Plates

# List of Figures

*From the author's original drawings except where otherwise indicated*

# List of Maps

MAP 4 (see p. 77)

*Sites mentioned in Chapter 4*

MAP 5 (see p. 113)

*Sites mentioned in Chapter 5*

Balance  5 Banleau  6 Beaussement  7 La Bergerie Haute etc.  8
Cambous  9 Camprafaud  10 Bovila de Can Torrents  11 Les
Cascades  12 Cerro de la Virgen  13 Châteauneuf-du-Pape  8
La Conquette  14 La Couronne  15 Dela-Laïga  16 Dorio  17
Embusco  18 Baume des Enfers, Grotte Basse  19 Estoublon and
Fontvieille  20 Eygalières  21 Grotta del Fico  22 Font-Juvenal
23 Francin  24 Gaudo  25 Grépiac  8 Janucq  26 Grotte de
Labeil  27 Lacabrette  28 Lagozza di Besnate  8 Lébous  29
Lévie  10 Bovila Madurell  30 Malaucène and Grotte Grangeon
31 Malta (Skorba, Ggantija, Mnajdra)  32 Los Millares  33
Monte d'Accodi  34 Monte Lazzo  35 Grotta Monte Maiore
36 Li Muri  37 Murs  38 Pagliaiu  39 Perpétiari  40 Perte du
Cros  41 Pescale  42 Peyro Blanco  6 Peyroche II  43 Grotta
dei Piccioni  26 Grotte des Pins  44 Praia dos Maçãs  5 Les
Rivaux  45 Rivoli  30 Roaix  46 La Romita di Asciano  47 St
Côme-et-Maruéjols  26 St Etienne-de-Gourgas  47 Salinelles  48
Grotta San Michele  49 Santu Pedru  50 Sargel I  38 Sartène
38 I Stantare  51 Toll de Moya  25 Toulouse area Sites (Auterive,
Blagnac, Mas Grenier, St Couffin, Châteauperçin)  11 Les Treilles
52 Le Verdier  53 Verdon Valley Sites (Grottes C, Murée and de
l'Eglise, Abri du Jardin du Capitaine)  54 Vila Nova de São Pedro
55 Zambujal

*Note:* The dates in this book are uncalibrated and based on the radiocarbon half-life of 5568. The convention 'b.c.' is used throughout to indicate radiocarbon years.

# 1 Introduction

This book covers developments in West Mediterranean Europe from the mid-seventh to the end of the third millennium b.c. (in radiocarbon years). The area covered by the book consists of Spain, Southern France, Italy, and the West Mediterranean islands. Some of these regions have been discussed in recent volumes in the *Ancient Peoples and Places* series (Spain and Portugal, Savory, 1968; Northern Italy, Barfield, 1971; Central and Southern Italy, Trump, 1966; Malta, Evans, 1959; Sicily, Bernabò Brea, 1957; Sardinia, Guido, 1963; and the Balearics, Pericot Garcia, 1972). This book will concentrate on the Southern French area, where the most comprehensive recent work on the West Mediterranean Neolithic has been carried out, and where quantities of radiocarbon dates now buttress the findings of stratigraphic excavations. The connections of Southern France down the Eastern seaboard of the Iberian peninsula, and along the Ligurian coast of Italy, will also be emphasized. Corsica and Sardinia have been intensively investigated in recent years, adding their individual stories to the multiplicity of developments in the early millennia of farming in the West Mediterranean.

Africa has been excluded, despite its proximity to Spain and Sardinia; to have included it would have expanded the text too far, and in any case the cultural connections of the two continents are either very limited (for example, North-West Morocco with Spain in the Early Neolithic – Souville, 1972, p. 68) or imperfectly understood (for example, North-West Africa with South-Eastern Spain in the late third millennium b.c.).

The plan of the book is to compare assemblages of very similar dates (in radiocarbon years) in order to establish some of the cultural and economic differences and similarities of contemporary prehistoric groups in West Mediterranean Europe. 'Culture' is used here to cover the characteristic artifacts and features of coeval human groups scattered over geographically contiguous areas, with

B

no single assemblage being regarded as typical. All the sites of a culture possess many, but not all, of its characteristics; the culture is polythetic (Clarke, 1968). It is assumed that the remaining artifacts and features reflect the activities of a given human society. Between two societies there will be 'edge areas', or zones where characteristic artifacts and features of both cultures are found (Gumerman, 1973).

With regard to economic strategy, in some cases good information is available in the shape of seeds and bones; in others assumptions must be made from artifacts or features or from a study of present-day land-use. Grahame Clark has recently re-emphasized that man and his way of life are the products of natural selection, and that 'natural selection has operated through the economic arrangements by which men have sought to extract a living from the world in which they live' (Clark, 1970, pp. 61–3). The information available from West Mediterranean Europe – admittedly partial and imperfect – seems to demonstrate slow but inexorable selection towards dependence on the products of domestication by about 2000 b.c. The dates used in this book are uncalibrated radiocarbon dates, based on the 5568 year half-life and indicated by the convention 'b.c.'

Calibration (or correction to absolute years B.C.) is not yet possible for the earliest dates, and there is dispute over the precise nature of the corrections that should be made to more recent ones. The original calibration curve by Suess produced the possibility that a single radiocarbon date might yield up to five calibrated dates because of the wiggles in the corrected line (Clark and Renfrew, 1972, p. 6); efforts to smooth out certain sections of this line have been partially successful but not universally accepted (Michael and Ralph, 1972; Clark and Renfrew, 1972; Ralph, Michael and Han, 1973; Damon, Long and Wallace, 1973; Switsur, 1973). In general, calibration of the dates given in this book will lengthen the span of time covered, for corrections vary from about 200 to 500 years around 2000 b.c. – a very difficult time period in radiocarbon terms – to 700–800 years around 4750 b.c. (Ralph, Michael and Han, 1973; Damon, Long and Wallace, 1973; Switsur, 1973).

The chronology given in this book is thus only an approximation of the truth; the span covered is probably more like 7500 B.C. to 2500 B.C. (in absolute years), and the resultant development of the farming way of life even slower than as viewed via the radiocarbon chronology. Sites with very similar radiocarbon dates should still be coeval, however, and their comparison has the advantage that typology can be left to play a cultural rather than a chronological

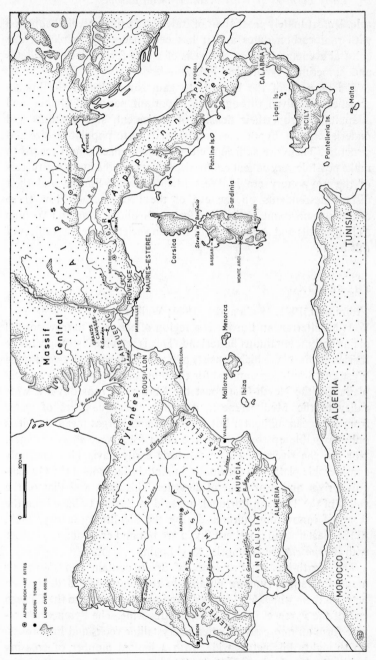

Map 1 (see p. 13)

role. Unfortunately great areas of Italy and Spain are still ill-supplied with radiocarbon dates and it has been necessary to place some cultural events in time on the basis of a very few radiocarbon dates and, sometimes, typological links.

The purpose of the book is to gain some idea of the human societies that lived through this important period of change and adaptation. From their density of settlement, site locations and material culture, hypotheses can be made as to population size and structure. There are sufficient clues in the archaeological record to make possible very cogent comparisons between the hunter-gatherers of the pre-pottery era in West Mediterranean Europe and their distant descendants on the eve of the Bronze Age. How these changes came about, and their effect on Neolithic Man and Woman as individuals and as members of human societies, are the subject of this book.

## THE SETTING

(Admiralty, 1941, 1942a and b, 1944; Walker, 1960)
West Mediterranean Europe is a region of generally narrow coastal plains and mountainous hinterland. This is seen most strongly in the Iberian peninsula, which consists of a vast plateau or *meseta* sloping West and South, surrounded for the most part by a narrow coastal plain. On the North-East coast the Ebro river runs down a wide valley to the Mediterranean, carrying great quantities of water from Pyrenean affluents; but its rapids and gorges mean that it is only navigable upstream from the coast for a very short distance. Nor are the rivers flowing westwards easily navigable. The only considerable plain is in the South, in Andalusia, around the Guadalquivir river and near mineral deposits. This area, and that of the valley of the Tagus in Portugal, are said by Savory to have been the scene of innovating cultures during the Neolithic (Savory, 1968, p. 18). Eastern and Southern Spain are hot and arid today; together with the *meseta* they comprise 'dry' Spain.

The North-Eastern provinces of Spain contain two *sierras* or mountain ranges running parallel to the coast, with a depression between them which has long been an important route to the Eastern end of the Pyrenees, only ten kilometres wide. The Pyrenees otherwise form an impressive barrier of crystalline rocks and limestones, up to eighty kilometres wide, with a limited number of crossing points. Major rivers such as the Garonne and Aude flow down the

Northern slopes into wide plains on the French side of the mountain barrier. The plain of Roussillon was formerly edged by lagoons and filled with swamps, and similar lagoon strands are found along the French Mediterranean coast as far as Provence. Behind the lagoons in Languedoc are gravel plateaux (*costières*) succeeded inland by foothills and plateaux of limestone now covered by spiny *garrigue* vegetation. The barren high limestone plateaux of the Grands Causses are riven by deep gorges, and to the North merge into the granite country of the Massif Central of France.

A break between Languedoc and Provence is provided by the valley of the Rhône river. The granites of the Massif Central run nearly up to its Western bank; from time to time the valley floor widens before it runs into the delta and out to the Mediterranean. To the East of the Rhône the limestones of the pre-Alps form the mountains of Lower Provence, scored by the gorges of rapid rivers like the Durance and its tributary, the Verdon. The Alps stretch for nearly 200 kilometres between France and Italy, lined by valleys leading to passes. Crystalline uplands near the Provençal coastline (Maures, Esterel) are relics of a mountain system now below sea level, but outcropping in Corsica and Sardinia. There is little or no coastal plain over much of the Riviera and Ligurian coastlines.

Italy is usually divided into the Northern continental, and Southern peninsula, zones. The former comprises the valley of the Po river, now restrained but formerly liable to flooding and marshes, and its surrounding alluvial fans, lakes and mountain ranges. From the Alps to the North streams feed into the Po, which flows to the sea near Venice. To the West and South the valley is blocked by mountain ranges (though there are low passes to the sea near Genoa) and the Alps merge into the pre-Apennines and Apennines.

The Apennine chain cuts off continental from peninsular Italy, and creates a central spine surrounded by narrow coastal belts to East and West. The mountains are cut by transverse valleys in Central Italy, but are more difficult to cross via the high Northern passes or the steep Southern ones. To the East there is a wide plain surrounding the present-day city of Foggia, partly cut off from the sea by the limestone plateau of the Gargano, an important source of flint.

As has already been stated, Corsica and Sardinia are predominantly formed of the same crystalline rocks (granites and schists) as the Maures and Esterel ranges of Provence. Both are predominantly mountainous islands, with seasonal streams. The straits of Bonifacio between the two islands are only twelve kilometres wide, and smaller islets dot the channel. Corsica is 183 kilometres long by eighty-three kilometres wide, and Sardinia 240 kilometres long by 120 kilometres wide. Sardinia's East coast is difficult of access, but along the North and West coasts there are several areas of plains; the biggest, the Campidano, leads from the South towards the volcanic area of Monte Arci in Central Western Sardinia.

All the countries of West Mediterranean Europe suffer from summer drought in the low-lying areas, and transhumance is a frequent reaction to the lack of feeding along the coasts in the summer months. Tree cover is generally sparse and the main flora is of drought-resistant plants. Game, particularly wild boar, can still be hunted in the mountainous back-country.

During the period covered by this book conditions in West Mediterranean Europe were rather different from today's. The mountain ranges were already established, but the recent alluvium of the river valleys had not yet accumulated (Vita-Finzi, 1969, p. 102). The sea-level was probably lower for at least part of the period (Gill, 1971, p. 2). In addition, ground cover was more complete than at the present time, and temperatures and humidity fluctuated considerably.

The period from 6500 b.c. to 2000 b.c. covers three main climatic divisions, the Boreal, Atlantic and Sub-Boreal. The Boreal climate was warm, and probably as dry as today; the Atlantic was slightly warmer and much wetter; and the Sub-Boreal wet and cool. These changes must have occurred very gradually and been hardly perceptible during the (short) individual life-span.

The seventh millennium b.c. may well have been a period of fairly extreme climatic behaviour. Carbon-14 dates suggest drastic flooding in the Garonne and Durance plains at the beginning of the millennium (Delibrias, Guillier and Labeyrie, 1974, p. 62), and the last eruptions of the Puy chain in the Massif Central occurred between the mid-seventh and mid-sixth millennia b.c. (Hassko, Guillet, Jaegy and Coppens, 1974, p. 121). From granulometric and sedimentological studies Escalon de Fonton and others have suggested that rockfalls occurred at the beginning of the Boreal in the La Madeleine cave, Montclus rock-shelter and Pertus 2 cave of Southern France (Escalon de Fonton, 1967).

The Boreal period begins in the early seventh millennium b.c. and persists until at least the mid-sixth millennium b.c. There is a date for peat from a Boreal level at Gumenil (Vosges) of 6020 b.c. (Hassko, Guillet, Jaegy and Coppens, 1974, p. 120). Level 16 at the rock-shelter of Montclus (Gard), marking the end of the Boreal, has been dated to 5590 b.c., and the Rouffignac site in the Dordogne seems to pass from the Boreal just prior to the level dated by radiocarbon to 5810 b.c. (Evin, Marien and Pachiaudi, 1973, p. 526 and Barrière, 1965a respectively).

However, there are other reasons for supposing that the Boreal continued until the opening centuries of the fifth millennium b.c. Hearth 7 at Châteauneuf-les-Martigues (Bouches-du-Rhône), climatically at the end of the Boreal, has been dated 4830 b.c. (admittedly in a new series of dates about a millennium earlier than previous dates for the same levels). Layer 8 at Montclus, 'at the end of the Boreal', has been dated 4280 b.c. (Evin, Marien and Pachiaudi, 1973, p. 526). A rock-shelter at Thoys, Arbignieu (Ain) has two dates for a Boreal level – 4240 and 4900 b.c.

It seems likely that warmer conditions developed by at least the mid-fifth millennium b.c. One of the revised Châteauneuf dates for the Atlantic Level 6 is 4480 b.c. (Ly 446). Shell-middens in the Marseille basin contain marine molluscs of species now emigrated to warmer waters (Fournier and Repelin, 1901). A check on charcoal fragments from hearths at Arene Candide, a cave on the Ligurian coast, suggests that the forest was increasing during the fifth millennium b.c., as the first pottery was acquired (Emiliani, *et al*, 1964, p. 139).

Pollen analyses from near Torreblanca, Castellon, Spain, suggest that a period of maximum humidity occurred about 4000 b.c. (Arribas, 1968). Palynological studies are relatively rare in France, but two useful studies have been carried out at the sites of Rouffignac and Châteauneuf-les-Martigues. At the porch site in front of the Rouffignac cave (Dordogne), Barrière has managed to combine pollen analysis and faunal determinations to suggest climatic and environmental change (1965a). The dry Boreal is represented by hazel and a few elm, with some oak, pine and willow, over an undergrowth of bracken and grasses (Barrière, 1965a, p. 8). Just before Level 3 (with its radiocarbon date of $5850 \pm 50 - GrN$ 2889) the proportion of trees declines. The mixed oak forest is more open, with a varied undergrowth, and includes lime, which does not grow in the area today (Barrière, 1965a, p. 9). In succeeding levels, down to the mid-fifth millennium b.c., lime decreases steadily and low plants increase.

The pollen diagram from Châteauneuf shows fluctuations within the Boreal and Atlantic periods (Renault-Miskovsky, 1971, p. 41).

The Boreal Levels 8 and 7 are mainly mild and dry, with an increase in humidity in the middle. The Atlantic levels have four oscillations corresponding to increases and decreases in tree-pollen and pollen of damp-loving species. The first period is mild and fairly damp (Level 6), the second fairly warm and fairly dry (Level 5), the third cooler and damp (Levels 4 and 3), and the last possibly drier (Levels 2 and 1 – Renault-Miskovsky, 1971, p. 41). The Sub-Boreal appears slightly warmer and very slightly damper than the final Atlantic (Level B).

Renault-Miskovsky concludes that the Mediterranean flora begins to establish itself in Provence during the Holocene, and is certainly visible in the Boreal; a true Mediterranean flora is established by the mid-Atlantic period, and pollen diagrams from North Italy in particular show this to have been a general phenomenon except in mountainous areas. The Italian diagrams emphasize the importance of the mixed oak forest in both the Boreal and Atlantic periods, with hazel as one of the components in the Boreal and holly or elm or pine in the Atlantic (Renault-Miskovsky, 1971, p. 40).

The Sub-Boreal begins sometime in the third millennium b.c. By this time a completely Mediterranean flora of pine, alder, *kermès* oak, pistachio, *Cupressaceae* and *Oleaceae* has been established at Châteauneuf, and pine, pedunculate and *kermès* oak, pistachio and *Cupressaceae* at the nearby site of La Couronne, dated by radiocarbon to the last half of the third millennium b.c. Renault-Miskovsky considers that the Sub-Boreal climate was very dry at this site, and that it finally forced the inhabitants to leave (Renault-Miskovsky, 1970, p. 118). A certain desiccation in some upland areas is suggested by the Late Neolithic vases found under temporary or permanent water-flows in 'cistern-caves' of the Grands Causses (Martin, *et al*, 1964).

Other techniques used in the Western Mediterranean include palaeotemperature analysis of the shells of marine molluscs, mainly *Trochus* and limpet. This method was applied to the Arene Candide stratigraphy, and suggested that the post-glacial temperature maximum occurred in Level 23 (*circa* 4500 b.c.). After this maximum temperatures dropped slowly to a minor maximum in Levels 13–14 (*circa* 2800 to *circa* 2000 b.c.), which should date the beginning of the Sub-Boreal (Emiliani, *et al*, 1964, p. 155).

Much more information, on an integrated basis, is required before the environmental changes of the final pre-farming and early farming eras of West Mediterranean Europe can be precisely tied down. The possibility of very varied weather patterns appearing simultaneously in neighbouring regions has been shown by a recent article on an analogue of the climate of Late Mycenaean Greece (Bryson, *et al,* 1974). In the meanwhile, individual sites have to be considered on the basis of faunal, mollusc and charcoal remains, which can give an idea of some of the surrounding environmental possibilities. The method of site catchment analysis can also suggest a range of economic strategies available to the occupants of individual sites (for example, Barker, 1974a).

The broad climatic changes of the period covered by this book must have been accompanied by local human alterations of the landscape. The process must have started from extremely small beginnings, clearings established by the sparse populations of pre-Neolithic hunters and gatherers. From the mid-sixth millennium b.c. in Southern France and Corsica (and later elsewhere) axes and sickles suggest that forest cover was broken in places to make way for cultivation or pasture. Renault-Miskovsky warns of this in analysing the Châteauneuf pollen sample, mentioning that herding of sheep was practised during much of the occupation of this site (Renault-Miskovsky, 1971, p. 38). Artistic representations of ploughing in Alpine valleys (Valcamonica and Mont Bego) suggest the presence of fields by at least the Late Neolithic. The period of this book encompasses a steady population rise and therefore a geometric increase in land usage. With very slow momentum the Mediterranean tree cover must have been pushed back around living sites, and the character of the Miocene limestone of which so much of the Mediterranean coast-lands are composed meant that surface drainage was swallowed up and the forest could not regenerate (Admiralty, 1942a, p. 119).

# 2 Pre-farming Communities

Farming does not take rapid hold on West Mediterranean Europe. From about 6500 b.c. to 5500 b.c. hunting and gathering economies predominate, though there are rare hints of sheep-herding and of grinding of stone. About 5500 b.c. the inhabitants of some coastal areas begin to use pottery and in some cases to herd animals. The first definite use of cereals is later. Many communities remain at least partly committed to the hunting and gathering economy until about 4500 b.c.

These pre-farming peoples – commonly called Mesolithic or Epipalaeolithic – occupied cave, rock-shelter and open-air sites, some of which are described below. In the main they are shadowy figures, whose rituals of songs and stories are unknown to us; a few, however, are portrayed in vigorous hunting scenes in Spanish rock art. They may have had skin clothing, and seem to have used body paint. Much of the year was probably spent in small groups of several families. Hunting of red deer and boar probably made close links between the male members of the group essential, leading to patrilocal residence after marriage. Women would have collected hazelnuts, acorns and other plant foods nearer to the camp. It seems likely that these groups were at least partly migrant, so that knowledge of varied environments and quarries, including large and small mammals, fish, birds and molluscs, would have been essential. People leading similar wandering lives in ethnographic situations are basically egalitarian, and the size of the residential group at any point in the annual cycle depends on the food source being exploited. It seems likely that Mediterranean Europe, like aboriginal California, was rich in possible food sources, and that by using the different environments men could eat well and multiply.

Mesolithic communities lived under pressure of change – of the climate, of sea-level, and of sources of food and shelter. In being adaptive, and in initiating change themselves, they made a contribution to Western civilization. Some sites seem to have been stable

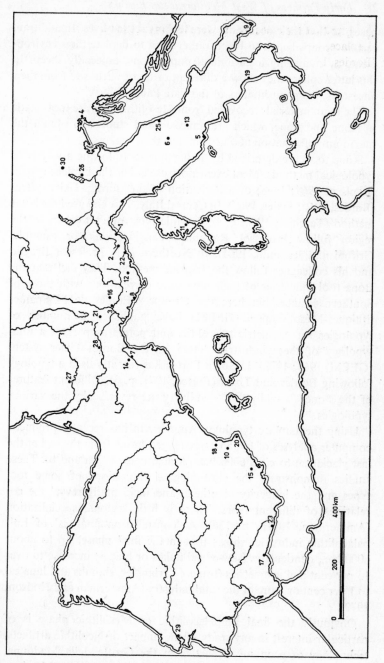

*Map 2 (see p. 13)*

bases, so that their occupants were leading settled lives. In addition, certain groups began to breed rather than to deplete their environment, by managing local animal populations, especially sheep. In this latter sphere they show a different order of virtuosity from their ancestors, the great hunters of the Late Palaeolithic.

The main materials recovered from Mesolithic sites are tools made in stone and bone, which are analysed and studied to obtain the maximum information about them and their makers.

Stone tools are described by archaeologists following a variety of typological methods. Most excavators use either the Laplace system (Laplace, 1964; 1968) or a derivation of the Bordes–Tixier system (Bordes, 1950; Tixier, 1963). In Central Italy, Taschini used the latter method (Taschini, 1968, p. 140), while most other workers in the region follow Professor Radmilli's classification (for example, Grifoni and Radmilli, 1964). In Northern Italy Professor Broglio and his colleagues follow the Laplace method. They feel that the stone tool industries of their area have correlations with those of Southern France, but here the Groupe d'Etudes de l'Epipaléolithiques-Mésolithiques (GEEM) have published a number of typologies for geometric microliths and points as part of a total typology of these industries based on the Bordes–Tixier system (GEEM, 1969; 1972). In Spain Fortea has recently used a typology following Bordes and Tixier (Fortea, 1971, p. 3). Different features of the stone – usually flint – industry are revealed by the various typologies.

Using the Laplace typology, Ammerman has recently produced computer analyses of Italian assemblages dating from the end of the last glaciation to *circa* 6000 b.c. (Ammerman, 1971a and b). These studies demonstrate the chronological limitations of some tool types and the longevity of others, and incidentally reveal the corelations of different types. There is little regional specialization (Ammerman, 1971a, p. 136). A 'constellation analysis' of Epipalaeolithic industries shows that in the final phase, up to about 6000 b.c., denticulates (saw-edged flakes or blades) increase to over 15 per cent and geometrics (trapezes, triangles, rhombs and lunates) to 1 per cent or more of the total industry (Ammerman and Hodson, 1972).

Obviously the final Epipalaeolithic or Mesolithic phase is of particular interest in any study of the impact of Neolithic artifacts, technology or economy. Apart from the Grotta della Madonna, most of the later assemblages considered by Ammerman and Hodson come from Northern Italy; indeed, Ammerman states that there is very little information about the latest Mesolithic in Southern Italy.

In a recent synthesis on the beginnings of the Italian Neolithic, Radmilli has emphasized two features, namely the persistence of stone tool types from pre-pottery to pottery levels at certain sites, and the possibly sedentary nature of Late Mesolithic shell-fish-based economies (Radmilli, 1972). Radmilli suggests that the upper levels of several Sicilian and Italian caves demonstrate a change to mollusc-collecting as a main economic strategy in the Late Mesolithic (Radmilli, 1972, p. 130).

The Grotta della Madonna, Praia a Mare (Calabria), which was excavated by 'spits' rather than cultural levels, has a date of 6785 ± 80 b.c. (R 187) for Levels 45-6 containing an industry of backed blades, short scrapers, borers, micro-borers and geometrics. These levels contain bones of red deer, roe deer, boar and ibex, with some increase of marine mollusc collection over previous levels (Cardini, 1970; Radmilli, 1972, p. 131). At the Apulian cave of Cipolliane di Novaghie a great number of marine molluscs are found in pre-pottery levels, together with stone tools, including geometric microliths, which continue into the overlying pottery strata (Peroni, 1967, pp. 42-3).

The majority of sites in Italy with late pre-farming levels occur in the Centre and North. In Central Italy most excavations have only taken place over a small area, and the quantities of lithic and faunal material are relatively low. Two of them, Porta di Positano cave and the Riparo Blanc rock-shelter, have produced mid-seventh millennium b.c. radiocarbon dates.

Porta di Positano cave, Positano (Campania), is dated 6669 ± 200 b.c. (Pi 10) (Ferrara, Reinharz and Tongiorgi, 1959, p. 106). The cave produced a microlithic industry, but no geometric forms. Its inhabitants appear to have collected marine and terrestrial molluscs and hunted ibex and boar (Taschini, 1968, p. 159).

The Riparo Blanc rock-shelter is located on the west flank of Monte Circeo (Taschini, 1964). It is cut into limestone and is about ten metres long by three metres wide. Charcoal distributed throughout the Mesolithic level was used to produce a radiocarbon date of 6615 ± 80 b.c. (R 341).

In the stratified level the most represented species of molluscs were winkles and *Trochus* (top shell). Many more molluscs were found in zones that had been disturbed. Numbers of *Columbella* shells had been perforated, presumably for use as pendants. Taschini links the mollusc exploitation to the formation of salt-water lagoons in the area following a rise in sea-level (Taschini, 1968, p. 139). Of the seventy-two lithic pieces found *in situ,* notches and denticulates accounted for nearly 60 per cent of the whole, while borers and side-scrapers were also well represented. Taschini wonders if the borers may have been used to open the bivalve shell-fish.

Faunal fragments found in disturbed ground were about ten times as numerous as those found *in situ*; in each group pig, roe deer and wolf are the most frequently represented, although the minimum number of individuals of each species is not reported (Taschini, 1964, pp. 70–1).

Other areas which were occupied by pre-farming peoples in Central Italy include the former lake basins of Fucino and Ofena in Abruzzo. The finds from the Fucino sites do not indicate any con-tinuity of occupation into the pottery-using period. However, at Ofena a drainage channel cut in 1965 revealed the site known as Capo d'Acqua. Excavations only took place over 9 m², but 456 flint tools and 642 waste flakes were recovered. The flint was locally obtainable from the silicious limestone around the basin (Tozzi, 1966, p. 15). 79 red deer bones and 64 wild cattle bones were identi-fied from the 2580 fragments found.

No radiocarbon date is available for Capo d'Acqua, but the excavator regards it as just prior to the Neolithic in the same area. A neighbouring site near one of the many springs produced Impres-sed Ware and pottery with wide red-painted bands, and a very similar lithic industry: 'despite the presence of obsidian and some typically Neolithic products, [the lithic industry] shows remarkable affinities with our industry' (Tozzi, 1966, p. 24). At the Neolithic site the sparse bone remains were predominantly of boar and red deer, followed by cattle and sheep-goat (Bonucelli and Faedo, 1968, p. 100).

Signs of Mesolithic occupation have also been found below the huts of the well-known Neolithic site of Ripoli (for example, Cremonesi, 1965, p. 91). Unfortunately there are insufficient finds for the possible relationships between the two occupations to be brought out. Fortunately a different situation prevails in part of North Italy.

Broglio has recently discussed the Epipalaeolithic of North Italy in several papers (Broglio, 1971; 1972). He distinguishes the Epi-palaeolithic of *circa* 6000 b.c. to *circa* 4500 b.c. in North Italy from the Epigravettian industries of prior to 8000 b.c. Unfortunately there is a gap in the succession before 6000 b.c., but from this time onwards a 'Sauveterroid' industry appears in the Adige valley area. At the Vatte di Zambana (Level 10) – carbon-14 date 6010/5910 b.c. (R490) – and at Romagnano III (Level AC-1), there are bilaterally backed points, backed blades and points with bilateral backing and oblique truncation, triangles, and more carinated scrapers and use of the microburin technique than in preceding industries (Broglio, 1972). The faunal determinations from these two sites indicate that hunting was popular at Vatte, while in addition to hunting the Romagnano dwellers collected large quantities of the lake mollusc *Unio* (Broglio, 1971, p. 187).

In Level AB-3 at Romagnano III trapezes and denticulates begin to come in, and in the succeeding Levels AB-2 and AB-1 there is a true 'Tardenoid' industry, with scalene, isosceles and rectangular trapezes produced by the microburin technique, and denticulated blades. In the same levels are plenty of roe deer bones and some marten and squirrel remains. *Unio* collecting gradually dies out in the AB levels. Perforated *Columbella* and *Neritina* shells are found in these levels, and incised bones – an awl and a metacarpal (Broglio, 1971, p. 172 and fig. 16 respectively).

Broglio likens the Tardenoid of the Adige valley to the Trieste carse finds at the Grotta Azzurra di Samartorza (Cannarella and Cremonesi, 1967). Here the Mesolithic layers contained 6560 artifacts, of which 2356 were tools. 53 blades or other tools were backed, there were 40 geometrics and 84 microburins, 102 borers or beaks, 158 scrapers and 19 burins. The geometric trapezes came in at Level F4 and increased over time. Long-bones of mammals or red deer antler were used to make points and chisels. Early Mesolithic economy was based on large mammal hunting and a little fishing, and limpet and top-shell collection began just before the development of microliths. By the end of the Mesolithic occupation shell-fish collection was a very important economic activity (Cannarella and Cremonesi, 1967, graph 1). The changes in economy and industry are said by the excavators to be slow and evolutionary. The Mesolithic sequence at Grotta Azzurra has been dated from 6000 to 5000 b.c. based on alterations in sea-level in the nearby Mediterranean.

On the West Italian coast, the famous Ligurian site of Arene Candide was occupied in the Early Mesolithic, not in the period preceding the first use of pottery (Cardini, 1946, p. 36). In the same area, the site of Arma dello Stefanin seems to have been occupied in the seventh millennium b.c.; the rather confusing series of dates run from 6450 and 6150 b.c. for the lower Levels Vb and Va (R148, R126) to 6850 and 5850 b.c. for Level IV (R145, R109). The flint tools consist mainly of scrapers, especially circular ones, and denticulates, and there is one obsidian scraper in Level V (Leale Anfassi, 1958–61). The animal most represented in the faunal record at all levels is the ibex, followed by boar and red deer. Various marine molluscs are found, especially mussel, and some of them have been bored for suspension as pendants or beads (Figure 1).

Another Ligurian cave with perhaps a later lithic assemblage – although no radiocarbon dates are available – is the Abri Mochi, one of the Grimaldi caves. In its upper level were backed points and bladelets, scrapers, burins, isosceles and scalene triangles, lunates and microburins (Barral and Simone, 1948, p. 102). Another lunate and a few backed bladelets were found associated with a crouched male burial, decorated with perforated shells, at Grotte du Rastel, Peillon (Alpes Maritimes) (Barral and Simone, 1968, p. 102). This rite is different from the elongated burials at the base of the Meso- lithic levels at Arene Candide (Cardini, 1946, fig. 3), and resembles closely the Early Neolithic burials both in Liguria and Southern France (for example, Figure 3:1).

No Mesolithic sites have been reported from Sardinia, and in Corsica most of the information comes from surface collections in the North of the island. However, Level VII at the site of Curac- chiaghiu, Lévie, in South-Western Corsica, has two radiocarbon dates, of 6610 and 6350 b.c. (Gif 1967 and 1963). Large cobbles of hard rock (possibly rhyolite) provided raw material to make small flakes and rare blades, and many large disc-like scrapers. The excavator, Lanfranchi, suggests that the quartz fragments found in the level may have been used both to make tools, for instance points, or as strike-a-lights (1973, p. 224). This is a very important site and will be mentioned in succeeding chapters.

In France the work of typologists has emphasized the evolutionary

*Figure 1. Pierced red deer teeth and mollusc shells from Arma dello Stefanin (Liguria). No. 1, deer canine; No. 2, pierced cervid femur; No. 3, Dentalium; No. 4, biconically pierced bead of large shell; No. 5, Pectunculus; No. 6, Cyclonassa; No. 7, Nassa critida; Nos. 8, 10, Columbella rustica; No. 9, Cerithium tuberculatum. Scale – natural size.*

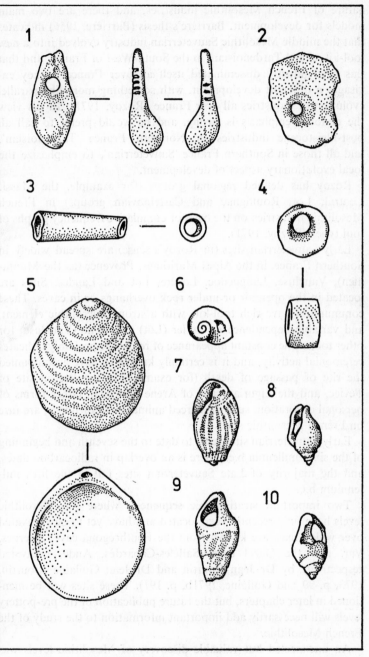

nature of French Mesolithic industries, and there are two main models for development. Barrière's thesis (Barrière, 1956) indicates that the middle Mesolithic Sauveterrian industry evolved into a new tool-kit, called Tardenoisian, in the South-West of France, and that this new industry disseminated itself all over France. Rozoy envisages a different development, with something more like parallel evolution of industries all over France (Rozoy, 1971). In his view the regional emphasis is strong, and he would prefer to call all post-Pleistocene industries in Northern France 'Tardenoisian', and all those in Southern France 'Sauveterrian', to emphasize the local evolutionary aspect of development.

Rozoy has defined regional groups (for example, the Massif Central, Lot, Rouffignac and Castelnovian groups) in French Mesolithic industries on the basis of cumulative frequency graphs of tool types (Rozoy, 1971).

Early Sauveterrian sites (in Rozoy's sense) are spread widely in Southern France, in the Alpes Maritimes, Provence (as the Montadien), Vaucluse, Languedoc, Lozère, Lot and Landes. Sites are located in the open air or under rock overhangs or in caves. These communities have rich tool-kits with a strong microlithic element, and variable dependence on antler (Lot) and bone (Vaucluse) for other tools. The constant appearance of red ochre probably indicates ceremonial activity, and it is certainly known to have accompanied the rite of passage of death (for example, in the Breton site of Téviec, and the Ligurian cave of Arene Candide). Other forms of personal decoration, such as pierced animal teeth or bones, are rare on French Mesolithic sites.

Early Sauveterrian sites seem to date to the seventh and beginning of the sixth millennia b.c.; there is an overlap in radiocarbon dates, and the majority of Late Sauveterrian sites fall in the fifth millennium b.c.

Two important stratigraphic sequences, where the Mesolithic levels have only recently been located and have yet to be excavated over wide areas, are known from the Fontbrégoua cave, Salernes, Var, and the Gazel cave, Sallèles-Cabardès, Aude, excavated respectively by Dr Jean Courtin and Dr Jean Guilaine (Courtin, 1973, p. 99 and Guilaine, 1971b, p. 191). These sites will be mentioned in later chapters, but the future publication of the pre-pottery levels will necessarily add important information to the study of the French Mesolithic.

An unexpected but valuable discovery of Mesolithic levels was made when the porch area of the Rouffignac cave was excavated. The first part of the report has just been published (Barrière, 1974). A trench 2–3 metres wide and 24 metres long was excavated to a depth of 6 metres (Barrière, 1974, p. 65).

The stratigraphy ran from Late Palaeolithic to modern times, and included five Mesolithic levels. Level 4, the earliest Mesolithic level, has three dates: 4a, $6420 \pm 100$ b.c.; 4b, $6640 \pm 95$ b.c.; 4c, $7045 \pm 105$ b.c. (GrN 2913, 2895 and 2880). Sauveterrian points and triangles were found at this level, together with dihedral and plan burins, and heavily backed and truncated 'knife-sickles', some with a sheen or lustre, presumably used for harvesting grasses (Barrière, 1974, p. 155). There was an evolution through the three horizons, 4c through 4a in the lithic industry (Barrière, 1965b, p. 159).

The wild boar was always the chief quarry of the dwellers at Rouffignac, and their activity reached a peak at the beginning of the seventh millennium, then slowly declined. Red and roe deer are present in the faunal remains in much lower quantities; the red deer increases steadily in importance throughout the seventh millennium, but still represents only 18% of the fragments as against the boar's 54·4%. However, the red deer is a heavier animal, and may well represent an important element in the diet. The published table only gives percentages of bone fragments recovered, however, and does not reveal the possible number of individual animals captured (Barrière, 1965a, p. 11). Barrière links the relative importance of boar and red deer at any given time to the climatic fluctuations, suggesting that the boar is important when there are parkland conditions, and the red deer when the forest spreads more densely.

Another site dated to the early seventh millennium b.c. is Les Salzets, Mostuéjouls (Aveyron) (carbon-14 date $6820 \pm 200$ b.c. – Maury, 1969). This site lies under a rock-shelter about 850 metres above sea-level on the Causse de Sauveterre. It is about 24 m² in area, and contains a single occupation 30 cm thick, consisting of broken bones, chipped flint and wood charcoal. All the chipped stone tools are under 1·5 cm long; they consist of points retouched on one or both sides, backed segments of circles and triangles going from the nearly equilateral to the very flared. Food debris is found in the form of half-burnt hazelnuts, and the bones of red deer, boar and aurochs.

An apparently rather later site has been excavated in the open air on a bend of the River Nesque in the Vaucluse (Paccard, 1971). This site, Gramari, has a radiocarbon date of 6050 b.c. for Level 3b and another of 5790 for Level 3a (Paccard, 1971, p. 83). The industry consists of triangles, microburins, a few backed bladelets and lots of heavy denticulated and notched tools on flakes, together with short small carenoid and denticulate scrapers. In Level 3a the excavations revealed two 'habitation units' of hearth-cum-pit areas of cobbles and charcoal (Paccard, 1971, fig. 20). One of these in Unit 2 is one metre in diameter and is suggested to have been used for indirect cooking (with stones laid on top of the braize). Other flatter areas of stones full of burnt material are more or less contiguous and in Unit 1. Three smaller hearths, and a circular post-hole surrounded by stones, were also found.

The first occupation area was distinguished from the second by a large quantity of faunal remains; the excavator regards the first as the butchering area, the second as a meat-drying and flint-working area. The post-hole, situated near to the hearth-free zone by the rock wall, may be the remains of a habitation structure beneath the overhang. A very similar arrangement of features is also known from the next lower level, 3c.

Planning of all faunal remains and snails and flints revealed a non-random distribution of remains over the site. The large denticulates and scrapers were associated with the faunal remains, and there were distinct knapping areas.

Red deer provided the majority of faunal remains, followed by boar, then large cattle in Levels 3a and 3b; in Level 3c sheep are more important than cattle. Paccard suggests that red deer, roe deer and boar were chased in the forest on the Nesque gorges, ibex on the slopes of Mt Vaucluse, and horse and cattle in the open grasslands of the Montmoiron–Carpentras plain. Rabbit and snail (*Helix nemoralis* and *Cyclostoma elegans*) were also found on the site in great numbers.

Paccard has excavated six other sites in the Vaucluse which reveal Mesolithic occupation from approximately the end of the Boreal onwards (rock-shelters of Roquefure, Chinchon II and III, Recougourdière, and Moure-de-Sève, and caves of Combe-Buisson and Unang – Paccard, 1954; 1963). This cluster of Vaucluse sites is of considerable interest for comparison with the stratigraphy established by Escalon de Fonton on the other side of the Rhône valley at the Baume de Montclus site in the Gard department.

The rock-shelter called Baume de Montclus is situated thirty-five metres above the river Cèze. It was excavated in the early 1960s by M. Escalon de Fonton, and the site report is in preparation. The stratigraphy, structural and archaeological remains have so far only been discussed in preliminary reports (Escalon de Fonton, 1966a; 1970b).

The stratigraphy consists of middle and late Mesolithic levels (Sauveterrian and Castelnovian, in Escalon's terminology), surmounted by Cardial and Chasséen. There are at least sixty layers of deposition, many of them with signs of structures. Most of the 'huts' appear to have been located in the Eastern part of the shelter, where the greatest protection is afforded (Escalon, 1966, p. 347). These 'huts' consist of a hearth located in a depression, occasionally with associated stones, and a single central post-hole. All types of lithic material are found in these depressions, plus fauna and bone tools. A plan has been published showing the distribution of finds in Hut 13D (Escalon, 1966, fig. 3).

Big hearths, and post-holes interpreted as holders for fish-drying racks, are found at all levels in the western part of the rock-shelter (Escalon, 1966, p. 349). The lithic industry in this area consisted exclusively of projectile points, often in groups of two or three.

Four very consistent carbon-14 dates are known from Levels 21F and 22, which contain Sauveterrian triangles and 'needles'. These are as follows

| | |
|---|---|
| Layer 21F (charcoal) | $5940 \pm 170$ b.c. (Ly-305) |
| Layer 21F (bone) | $5830 \pm 250$ b.c. (Ly-306) |
| Layer 22 (charcoal) | $5820 \pm 410$ b.c. (Ly-307) |
| Layer 22 (bone) | $5800 \pm 340$ b.c. (Ly-308) |

A date for Level 22 from another laboratory is some three hundred years earlier – $6180 \pm 240$ b.c. (KN-58).

It is impossible to generate percentages of the raw materials used at this site, since full publication has yet to be made, but presumably chipped stone remains are in the majority, with bone perhaps second, while shell, colouring material and cobbles would be brought to the site in differing quantities. On the economic side, Escalon de Fonton reports that nearly all the bones found in the site were of fish, plus a few wild cat. It seems likely to the excavator that the Montclus rock-shelter was a temporary camp, most likely in the summer when the Cèze waters would be low, and clear for fishing (Escalon, 1970a, p. 108).

At Montclus the trapeze is added to the lithic inventory in Levels 15 and 16; Level 16 has recently been dated $5590 \pm 160$ b.c. (Ly-542). At Rouffignac the trapeze is found in Level 3, together with Sauveterrian points, muzzled scrapers and some poor burins, dated 5810 b.c.

Level 3 at Rouffignac contains eleven hearths and faunal remains of 47·4% wild boar, 27·7% red deer, and 8·3% each roe deer and domesticated dog (Barrière, 1965, p. 11).

Many more sites in Southern France were associated with fishing or gathering activities. Louis, the last person to publish a general synthesis of the Languedoc–Roussillon area, called the Mesolithic occupation 'la culture des sables', in response to the relatively common location of microlithic industries around beaches and lagoons (Louis, 1948). In the Garonne valley riverside sites of considerable size seem to have been occupied continuously since the Late Mesolithic (Galy, 1971), presumably pursuing a rewarding fishing economy. The La Cauna cave, Arques, Aude, produced an archaeological level thick with *Helix nemoralis* shells and a few backed microliths including a lunate, plus a few choppers (Sacchi, 1971, figs. 1–3).

New dates for the Châteauneuf-les-Martigues stratified rock-shelter site place the final Mesolithic (called Castelnovien after this site-type by its excavator, Escalon de Fonton, 1956) in the sixth and early fifth millennia b.c. (5880 to 4830 b.c. – Ly 438, 448/624). The surviving raw materials from the Castelnovien levels consist solely of chipped flint, bone, antler, ochre, sea-shells and cobbles from marine alluvions. The lithic industry changed gradually over time: a basically heavy component, matched with lighter bladelets, often truncated, and microburins, gradually acquired more regularly shaped trapezes, flat scrapers on flake-blades, and borers (for example, Escalon de Fonton, 1956, fig. 29.7).

The economic strategy for this site seems to have included hunting and possibly herding of sheep (Ducos, 1958); Ducos' suggestion that sheep were partially domesticated in the Late Mesolithic is of great importance for West Mediterranean European prehistory. Similar animal management has only rarely been suggested (Davidson *in* Walker, 1972; Barker, 1974a) and must presumably be dependent on the exploitation potential of a particular site and the degree of stability of its inhabitants.

Sheep were only one of the quarries of the inhabitants of Châteauneuf; many rabbit bones are found in Late Mesolithic levels, and the relative frequency of the four main species based on the number of individuals is as follows: sheep 40·8%, red deer 25·9%, boar 22·2%, cattle 11·1% (Murray, 1970, table 16).

In Spain the pre-pottery levels of the caves in the Barcelona region have not been clearly defined, but further down the Eastern coast the lithic industry of the Cocina cave at Dos Aguas has recently been re-interpreted (Fortea, 1971). Using radiocarbon dates from the Portuguese Tagus sites (to be discussed shortly), Fortea suggests that the first Epipalaeolithic or Cocinese I industry stretches from approximately 6200 to 5400 b.c. This industry contains scalene and other triangles, many trapezes and notches, burins, backed bladelets and scrapers, and a macrolithic element. It is followed by the Cocinese II industry, where the macrolithic tools disappear, and the micro-burins put in an appearance. At this time (*circa* 5080 to 4100 b.c. according to Fortea), trapezes, notched tools and denticulates are relatively frequent. Also present at this level were many pebbles incised with rayed designs (Pericot, 1945, lamina III). The succeeding Cocinese III level has much the same lithic types, but in reduced quantity, with backed bladelets, and lunates and isosceles and scalene triangles; *Cardium*-impressed and incised pottery accompany the lithic industry.

What was claimed to be a 'great quantity' of shell remains were obtained during Pericot's excavation in the 1940s at this cave (appendix by Vidal y Lopez, Pericot, 1945, p. 32). However, the malacologist identified only about thirty molluscs in his preliminary report, including marine, lake-side and terrestrial varieties (Vidal y Lopez, Pericot, 1945, p. 33). Davidson has indicated that the Meso-lithic economy was based on hunting of goat, deer and horse (Davidson, 1972, p. 26).

This coherent picture of the evolution of the lithic industry is apparently visible elsewhere in the Valencia region (Fortea, 1971, p. 87). Backed bladelet industries, although without geometrics, appear in Cueva de les Mallaetes and Cueva de les Rates Penaes, below pottery levels; sheep have recently been identified in the pre-pottery levels at the former (Davidson, quoted in Walker, 1972, p. 14). At the Covacha de Llatas all the layers contained crescentic and geometric flints, burins, scrapers and unretouched blades, and only the topmost layer also produced pottery. Walker has recently linked these sites with the Abrigo Grande in the Segura river basin, Murcia, where a microlithic industry in Level 3 (backed bladelets and points, lunate, end scraper and pyramidal cores) was succeeded by a similar lithic industry accompanied by plain sherds of deep-handled bowls and jugs in Level 2 (Walker, 1972, p. 5 and figs. 13–14). Mollusc shells are found in both levels. Rabbit, boar, red deer, and horse bones appear in both levels, with the addition of caprines and cattle in Level 2 (Walker, 1972, p. 22).

Abrigo Grande is next door to a rock-shelter decorated with

anthropomorphic and zoomorphic painted figures. The anthropomorphs are variously stick figures or thickened in outline, for instance as though wearing skirts. Red deer, ibex, boar and sheep seem to be illustrated (Walker, 1972, fig. 2).

'Levantine' rock-painting (stretching down the mountain zone of Eastern Spain from Catalonia to Murcia) has recently been briefly synthesized by Savory (Savory, 1968). These exposed drawings are mostly of wild animals (cattle, red deer, fallow deer, ibex, boar) and there are a number of hunting and other scenes. Despite the views of certain writers (for example, Jorda, 1966) that these artistic manifestations can all be dated to the Neolithic, Savory believes that it is all post-glacial, and extends to the arrival of the first farmers about 5000 b.c. and a little beyond (Savory, 1968, p. 57). The later pictures are usually the most schematic, and even include agricultural and axe-brandishing scenes. The successful economy which presumably made this art-form possible may have delayed acceptance of farming traits in the Spanish hinterland, and will certainly have affected their development.

The coherent evolutionary picture of lithic industries demonstrated for the Valencia area is rarely visible in the rest of Spain. However, in the province of Málaga two cave excavations suggest a rather similar picture. At Hoyo de la Mina cave the pre-pottery levels contained backed tools, end and side-scrapers and carinated scrapers, and borers, associated with 95% mollusc (mussel) and 5% wild animal remains, belonging to boar, ibex, rabbit, cattle and dog (Arribas, 1972, p. 125).

At the large Nerja cave Pellicer discovered pre-pottery levels in three trenches in different parts of the cave (Belen VII and VIII, Cascada V and Fantasmas III – Pellicer, 1963, p. 33). Only the first two trenches gave any real, if sparse, indication of this occupation: the Mesolithic people had left small unretouched blades and flakes and a possible burin (Pellicer, 1963, fig. 20.2), together with shell-fish remains, and, in the Belen gallery, bones of birds and small rodents. The small fauna and shell-fish continued to be exploited in the succeeding pottery Level VI.

The Mesolithic period in Iberia has long been associated particularly with the shell-middens of the mouth of the Tagus in Portugal. Excavations by the Abbé Roche have taken place in the lower levels of Moita do Sebastião (the upper levels had been razed for a housing development), through thirty-nine levels of deposit at Cabeço da Armoreira, and most recently at Cabeço da Arruda.

Roche has emphasized that these shell-middens were formed in a particularly favourable environment. They are found on the edge of the Tagus estuary at what was the confluence of fresh and salt water, in an area where bovids and cervids were near enough to hunt, and where many types of aquatic birds migrated in the autumn (Roche, 1972, p. 72). Most of the shell-fish species encountered in the midden are known in the area at the present day, but several pincers of *Gelasimus tangeri,* a type of crab now found further South, suggest a slightly warmer water temperature than at the present day (Roche, 1965, p. 137).

The Moita do Sebastião site produced a flint industry predominating in denticulates and geometrics (especially trapezes), with many used and retouched flakes and some microburins (Roche, 1972, p. 87). Both the flint industry and the heavier quartz industry were analysed by the Laplace method. The trapezes are typically very elongated or virtually tanged. Antler was used for borers and polishers, and there were also bone borers. Pierced stones and shells and fragments of the colourant haematite are sometimes found associated with the burials; Roche excavated thirty-four skeletons including children buried in individual pits, while adults were apparently laid crouched on the ground and then covered. Many other burials had been reported from previous excavations.

Other features of the Moita excavation were sixty-one post-holes possibly representing semi-circular huts or wind-breaks, and a trapezoidal ditch with river cobbles at its base. There were also nineteen cooking holes, and two storage pits with unopened shell-fish still piled in them. The 20 cm of deposit left at this site was dated by radiocarbon to $5400 \pm 350$ b.c. (Sa-16 – Roche, 1972, p. 94).

The excavations at Cabeço da Armoreira are valuable in that they demonstrate an evolution in the lithic industry – geometrics increase in importance, with triangles becoming proportionately much more frequent than trapezes. Denticulates, retouched flakes and used flakes gradually reduce in importance over time. Microburins, on the other hand, increase. Roche suggests that the triangles are an end-product of gradual elongation of the trapezes (Roche, 1972, p. 91). Level 39 – the bottom level – is dated $5080 \pm 350$ b.c. (Sa-195) and Levels 3–4 near the top of the midden $4100 \pm 300$ b.c. (Sa-194) (Roche, 1965, p. 137).

Unfortunately both Cabeço da Armoreira and Cabeço da Arruda were excavated by trenching, which has enabled the excavator to establish the stratification of these very complex sites (there were eighty-two levels at Cabeço da Arruda), but which militates against the kind of interesting plans of pits and ditches produced in the Moita excavation. No hut floors were detected at Cabeço da Armoreira, although pits and hearths were detectable both here and on the opposite bank of the Muge.

Cabeço da Arruda has produced a very small quantity of lithic material, but quite a variety of worked bone and antler in the form of chisels, points, sleeves, and 'axes' (Roche, 1972, p. 92–3). Charcoal from Levels 71–82 has produced a radiocarbon date of 4480 ± 300 b.c., and the final occupation is dated by charcoal from Levels 3–6 at 3200 ± 300 b.c. (Roche, 1972, p. 94). If the latter date is correct it would suggest continuity of the Muge shell-midden lifestyle well beyond the time when the first pottery was introduced into Portugal and when the first megalithic tombs were built.

Unfortunately there are no column samples to indicate possible change in mollusc species utilization over time at the Muge sites. The majority of marine shells fall into the species of *Cardium edule, Scrobicularia plana* and *Neritina fluviatilis*; terrestrial molluscs were different species of *Helix* (*pisana, virgata, acuta, apicina*). Bird and fish bones, of varieties known in the area today, are also reported without any quantification. Equally there are no minimum numbers of individuals for the boar, red and roe deer, wild cattle and small mammal remains. Any development of the economy over time is thus obscured; however, Roche does maintain that preliminary analyses reveal little difference between the fauna from the three different sites, so that any change would seem to have been proportional rather than of a drastic nature (Roche, 1972, p. 85).

The above description of a number of Mesolithic communities of the seventh and sixth millennia b.c. has revealed that there was a common fund of stone tools, manufactured in varying proportions in different regions. However, these regions are very extensive (as witness Rozoy's contrast of the development of Mesolithic industries in North and South France).

Scrapers, denticulates, borers and burins are found fairly generally over time and space. It seems likely that the first two are to be linked with the preparation of hides and meat (for example, Gramari), the borers possibly with the exploitation of shell-fish, and the burins with the making of other tools. Regional variation occurs with the triangle, which is found in the earlier Mesolithic of Northern Italy and Southern France. In Northern Italy it is found stratigraphically earlier than the trapeze. The trapeze makes its appearance about the mid-sixth millennium b.c. both here and in Spain and France; it does not spread into Southern Italy. Elongated triangles, possibly locally derived from the trapeze, replace this latter form in Spain and Portugal, probably in the late fifth millennium.

While common traditions of Late Palaeolithic stone tool manufacture followed by similar economic activities may account for the general similarities in Mesolithic industries, the wide regional similarities suggest that human groups were active over large territories. Australian tribes wandered over territories of up to 6000 square miles (Yengoyan, 1968, p. 191), and half a dozen such groups could account for the Mesolithic occupation of Southern France. The more local variations in stone tool types noticed by Rozoy within the Southern French zone would reflect the particular craftsmanship of these groups. Geographical, not human, barriers seem to be the only factors to account for the different triangle and trapeze traditions, in the present state of our knowledge about the West Mediterranean Mesolithic.

# 3 The First Farmers

During the sixth millennium b.c. the sea makes its first vital contribution in produce and in communications in the Western Mediterranean. Radiocarbon dates reveal that by 5500 b.c. a lively economy had grown up in the Bay of Marseille, where fishermen ventured out in some of the first boats to travel on the Mediterranean. These particular communities also used pottery, which may well have been invented locally. Did they need extra storage facilities other than pits or baskets? Or did the sedentary nature of the successful marine-based economy permit experiments to be made resulting in these containers? Whatever the origin of the pots, the use of *Cardium* or cockle-shell to impress designs on their surfaces emphasizes and reiterates the importance of the sea and its resources in the lives of these small coastal groups.

The first West Mediterranean peoples to use pottery and ground stone axes very often continued to use the same types of bone and stone tools as their ancestors or predecessors. Ground stone querns, for instance, were found in Late Mesolithic contexts. Often the pottery-makers occupied the same cave or rock-shelter sites, and in some cases a long evolution in flint tool types and economy can be seen. Elsewhere new open-air sites were occupied near lagoons and lakes.

The development of lagoons and changes in sea-level during the sixth and fifth millennia b.c. provided extensive opportunities for an easy, year-round food supply. Molluscs can be collected from various tidal zones, but in no case is much specialized knowledge, strength or catching ability involved. Any member of the family can be employed. Such a food source provides a stable, if monotonous, diet, with a permanent sedentary base, leaving open the possibility of experimenting with other sea resources, land mammals or even planted crops. There are no signs of more elaborate social structures among groups using pottery, but it is possible that a more secure economy encouraged the slow growth of larger populations.

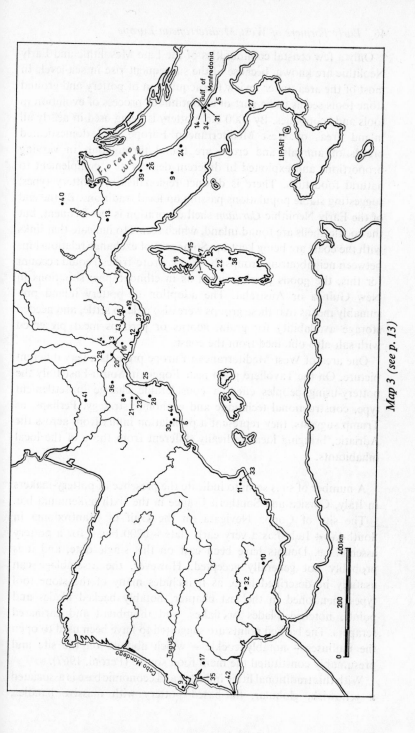

Map 3 (see p. 13)

Only a few coastal communities of the Late Mesolithic and Early Neolithic are known, because of the subsequent rise in sea-level. In most of the area under review the acquisition of pottery and ground stone tools seems to be part of a continuous process of evolution in tools and economies. By 4000 b.c. pottery is being used in nearly all inland areas of West Mediterranean Europe, and domesticated breeds of animals and crops are found throughout, in varying proportions and exploited in different degrees as a complement to natural foodstuffs. There is distinct regionalism of pottery types, suggesting stable populations passing on local traditions. By the end of the Early Neolithic *Cardium* shell decoration is less frequent, but the cockle-shells are found inland, which seems to indicate that links with the coast are being kept up. Some sort of exchange relationships between neighbouring groups (bands or 'proto-tribes') could account for this, the goods passing much as in ethnographic situations in New Guinea or Australia. The adoption of pottery inland presumably means that these groups were also able to settle, and needed storage availability for grain, acorns or perhaps meat preserved with salt also obtained from the coast.

One area of West Mediterranean Europe presents a very different picture. On the Tavoliere plain near Foggia in South-East Italy the pottery-using peoples effect a considerable change in settlement type, constructional technique and economic strategy. Perhaps, as Trump suggests, they represent a population influx from across the Adriatic, bringing ideas radically different from those of the local inhabitants.

A number of sites seem to indicate the presence of pottery-makers in Italy, Corsica and Southern France in the sixth millennium b.c. The site of Coppa Nevigata on the Gulf of Manfredonia in South-~~West~~ *East* Italy has a very early date – 6200 b.c. – for a pottery assemblage. Doubts have been cast on this single date, and it is probably not generally accepted. However, the assemblage can usefully be described here, as it includes many of the stone tool types mentioned in the last chapter, notably backed blades and points, notched blades or flakes, and thumbnail and carinated scrapers. The backed points are suggested to have been used to open the molluscs – notably cockle – which abound on the site and presumably constituted the main food source (Peroni, 1967).

With this traditional lithic industry and economic base is associated a yellowish, globular, flat-based pottery with massive handles, decorated with impressions of fingers, sticks or cockle (*Cardium*) shell. Polished stone is also present in the form of little steatite cylinders, one bored along all its length, perhaps for use as a bead. Other similar sites are found in some numbers in the Gulf of Manfredonia near lakes and lagoons (Radmilli, 1962).

Another site in South-West Italy, the Grotta Madonna above Praia a Mare, has a date of 5605 ± 85 b.c. Unfortunately the charcoal which gave this date came from two Levels 40 and 41, containing respectively the last Mesolithic and earliest Impressed Ware assemblages (Ammerman, 1971a, p. 381). There is thus no surety that the date refers to the first Neolithic occupation of the cave.

In Corsica, two sites have better associated mid-sixth millennium dates, Basi and Curacchiaghiu. Basi is a slight eminence near Filitosa in South-West Corsica. Quarry workings revealed prehistoric pottery and flint tools in 1965. The first occupation of the site took place during the Neolithic, and the lowest deposit, Level 7, Site 1, is dated to 5750 ± 150 b.c. (Gif 1851 Bailloud, 1972). This lowest deposit produced *Cardium*-impressed sherds from round-based bowls and jars, and a single vase with red paint associated with the impressed design (Fig. 3:1). The lithic industry was mainly on flint, but included 15 quartz and 10 obsidian fragments; the arrowheads were all transverse and marginally retouched. A single quern and one fragment of polished axe were found. Daub suggests that the first pottery-users at Basi lived in mud-walled huts, and from the faunal analysis it is known that they raised sheep (Bailloud, 1969, p. 383).

The other site, Curacchiaghiu (Lévie), is a rock-shelter with three sixth-millennium dates. Level VIc has been dated to 5650 ± 180 b.c. (Gif, 1962), and VIa to 5360 ± 170 (Gif, 1961) and 5350 ± 160 (Gif) (Lanfranchi, 1972). Unlike the contemporary Basi site, *Cardium*-impressed sherds are rare – only four were found – and most of the pottery bears lines of punctuate or incised design. The pottery is all round-based; a deep bowl with little lobes along the rim bears horizontal rows of incision below the rim, from which hang rough swathes (Lanfranchi, 1973, fig. 19); and necked globular jars with repair holes bear a decoration of two rows of punctuations around the shoulder, with dotted triangles rising above them (Figure 2:8). Some of the pots have handles with raised appendices. The lower level of rock-shelter D′ at Filitosa represents a lengthy Neolithic occupation, according to its excavator, Atzeni (1966), and contains a few *Cardium*-impressed sherds, plus bowls decorated with lines of incision, slight cordons or punctuate impression (Figure 3:9–11).

There are thus at least two early Neolithic pottery facies in Corsica (one with *Cardium* decoration dominant and one with punctuate decoration dominant – Lanfranchi, 1973, p. 220). Unfortunately no bones were preserved in the acid conditions of the Curacchiaghiu cave, which prevents a comparison being made with the sheep-herding economy of Basi. One quern was found at Curacchiaghiu, together with tools in obsidian and hard rock; transverse arrowheads, trapezes and lunates were produced in obsidian, and rectangular trapezes in hard rock (Lanfranchi, 1973, figs. 26A and B). Samples of the obsidian show that it originated in Sardinia (Hallam, Warren and Renfrew, in preparation) and it thus represents the earliest dated instance of trade between the two islands.

Three sites in Southern France have pottery levels dated to the sixth millennium b.c. They are the coastal sites of Cap Ragnon and Île Riou, both in the bay of Marseille, with dates of $6020 \pm 150$ and $5700 \pm 150$ b.c. (MC 500M, 500P – Courtin, 1974 in press), and $5650 \pm 150$ and $5420 \pm 160$ b.c. (MC 428/9) respectively. In addition, the rock-shelter of Châteauneuf-les-Martigues facing the Berre lagoon produced a date of $5570 \pm 240$ b.c. when material from Hearth 5 was dated at Cologne. However, this date can now be refined (Freundlich, personal communication). A new set of dates from Lyon – all but one in good agreement with their stratigraphic provenance – suggest that pottery was not used in this rock-shelter until the fifth millennium b.c. (Evin, Marien and Pachiaudi, 1973, p. 527).

The earliest dates for a site with pottery in Southern France (6020 and 5700 b.c.) come from the coastal cave site of Cap Ragnon near Marseille (Courtin, *et al* 1970–2). The archaeological material is scarce (*Cardium*-impressed sherds, a thick flake industry, bone piercer and chisel, and laterally-pierced *Columbella* shells). The economic information, however, has been fully developed. Some red deer, rabbit and sheep bones are recorded, but the predominant emphasis was on fish and molluscs. The fish caught were tunny,

---

*Figure 2. Corsican Early Neolithic (after Bailloud, Lanfranchi, Atzeni). Nos. 1–6 from Basi (note red painting over impressed triangles in No. 1); No. 7 from Araguina; No. 8 from Curacchiaghiu; Nos. 9–11 from Abri D', Filitosa. Scale – Nos. 1–6, one-third natural size; Nos. 7–11, half natural size.*

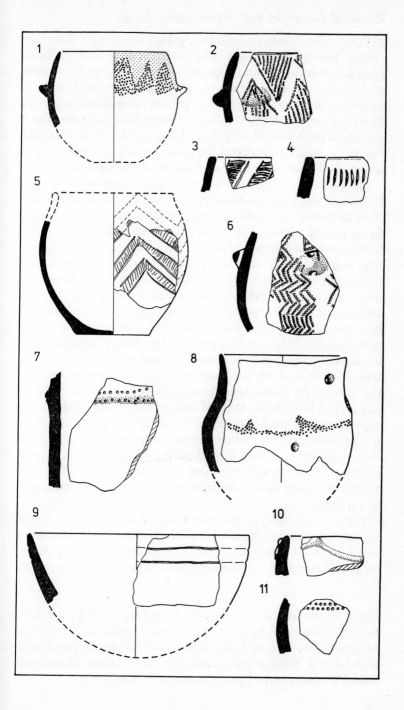

grouper, wrasse, sargus, seabream, porgy, moray and little Sela-
chians. Tunny-fishing might have involved using lines or boats.
Shell-fish consumed were topshell, limpet, dog-whelk, mussels,
spider-crabs and sea urchins. None of the faunal, land-snail, sea
mollusc or fish species were different from those found at present,
though the shell-fish *Patella ferruginea* was more frequent than at
present in the Marseille area (Courtin, *et al,* 1970–2, p. 161). This
interesting report gives one of the fullest accounts of the variety of
sea and land food enjoyed by an Early Neolithic community.

The Île Riou, off Marseille-Veyre, has been known as an archaeological site since the last century, but much of the occupation has
been destroyed by sand-quarrying. In 1968 Courtin and Froget
found part of a hearth still *in situ* in the shell-midden. *Patella* were
used to obtain the carbon-14 dates given above. The assemblage was
tiny, but included a marginally retouched transverse arrowhead, a
laterally pierced *Columbella* and a fragment of haematite. In addition
there were a large number of querns, and a globular pot with two
vertically perforated lugs and *Cardium* impression. Two other sherds
bore respectively a thick button, pierced horizontally, and a horizontal cordon. The querns were in a Quaternary sandstone now
found only below tide-level at Île Riou, and this has led to sugges-
tions that the sea-level was lower in the mid-sixth millennium, and
that perhaps Île Riou formed a peninsula of the mainland (Courtin
and Froget, 1970, fig. 4). It would seem inherently likely that a larger
expanse of land would be needed for cereal growing if in fact the
querns were used for grain-grinding. However, as at Skara Brae,
they may have been used for pulverizing fish-bones, if, as Courtin
claims, the site was a fishing camp (Courtin, 1972a, p. 118). Fish-
bones were found there in the nineteenth century (Fournier, quoted
by Courtin).

There are no traces of an earlier occupation on Île Riou, though
this cannot, of course, be ruled out – the evidence has been quarried
away. The shell accumulation must have been produced either by
the people using the *Cardium*-decorated pottery or their precursors.

---

*Figure 3. Neolithic Burials. No. 1, Arene Candide (Liguria) Early
Neolithic burial (after photograph of reconstruction in Genoa-Pegli
Museum); No. 2, Can Vallès (Catalonia) 'pit grave' burial (after
Guilaine and Muñoz); No. 3, Escanin 2, Les Baux (Bouches-du-
Rhône) Chasséen burial (after photograph by Montjardin).*

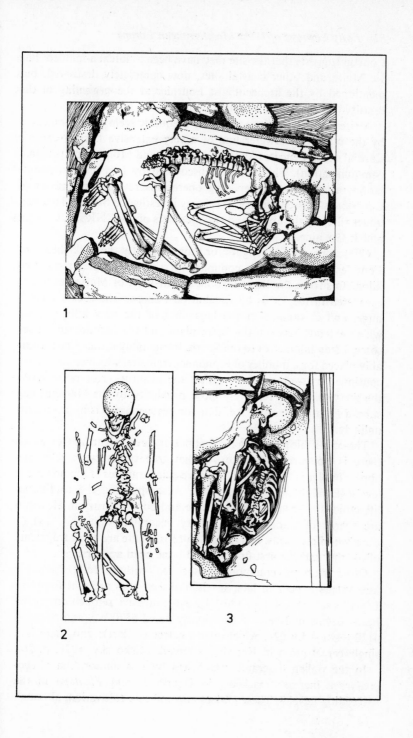

1

2

3

Courtin suggests that the site may have been a 'kitchen-midden' like Île Maire and other coastal sites, now completely destroyed, but mentioned by the archaeologist Fournier at the beginning of the century (Fournier and Repelin, 1901).

A rise in sea-level since the Early Neolithic seems to be indicated by the recent underwater find of a very extensive Early Neolithic Cardial site at Leucate (Aude) (FAH, 1973 and Montjardin, personal communication). This site was discovered by Freisses and Montjardin, after channel deepening operations revealed quantities of *Cardium*-impressed pottery. It is being investigated both on land and underwater by the above and two members of the CNRS, J. Courtin and J. Guilaine.

Châteauneuf-les-Martigues, or more correctly the rock-shelter of Font les Pigeons in the commune of that name, lies some two kilometres from the Berre lagoon, North-West of Marseille. It was excavated in the 1950s by Escalon de Fonton. The rock-shelter is huge, and is situated at the beginning of the very hilly country which extends between the Berre plain and the Mediterranean sea some fifteen kilometres to the South. Presumably it was thus favourably placed for a number of economic strategies, which seem to have continued a steady evolution after the acquisition of pottery. As the site was in such relatively close proximity to the Marseille bay sites, a sixth millennium b.c. date for pottery usage is by no means unlikely.

The only lithic change in the first pottery level, Hearth 6 (for which there is no carbon-14 date), is that true transverse arrowheads appear in place of the slightly concave-sided trapezes of the preceding levels (Escalon de Fonton, 1956). Accompanying the traditional lithic industry, beach cobbles, ochre and bone industry in Hearth 6 are sherds of smooth-faced pottery decorated with nail, awl or *Cardium*-impressions, and plastic buttons. There are a few fragments of querns, and the first flat polished bone bead appears.

Other features commonly associated with a fully Neolithic assemblage appear in later levels. Polished axes are first found in Level 6 (new date $4480 \pm 140$ – Ly 446); invasive retouch on arrowheads begins in Hearth 5 (previously dated 5570 b.c. and re-dated $4120 \pm 490$ – Ly 623, which seems extremely late); and there is a single cereal grain in Hearth 3 (Renault-Miskovsky, 1971, p. 36).

In the pollen diagrams established by this author, the *Chenopodiaceae* increase markedly in Hearth 3, and *Plantago* in the succeeding Level 3. These grasses may indicate cultivation, although this is not always the case in North-West Europe (Dennell, personal communication).

In the first pottery levels, as far as structural evidence is concerned there are no pits or other features; however, the wall of the shelter is painted with ochre in Level 6. The faunal evidence is not available by level, but the change from Late Mesolithic to Early Cardial brings about a marked reduction in the percentage of fragments of rabbit (94·7% to 58·5%) and an increase in the percentage of fragments of sheep (1·8% to 27·4%) (Ducos, 1958). The relative frequency of the four main species based on the number of *individuals* is as follows – sheep 52·2%, wild cattle 20·8%, boar 16·7% and red deer 10·4% (Murray, 1970, table 16). The status of the sheep in the Mesolithic is referred to by Ducos as 'imperfect domestication' (Ducos, 1958, p. 133); presumably the greatly increased number of fragments and the percentage increase of individuals in the Early Cardial Neolithic reflects a continuation of, and possible improvement in, this domestication process.

The majority of Cardial culture dates fall in the fifth millennium b.c. There are actually sequences of dates at some sites, for instance Abri 3 of St Mitre (Reillanne, Basses Alpes), where the Cardial Level 3 has dates for its bottom, middle and upper parts of 4750, 4450 and 4150 b.c. respectively (Guilaine and Calvet, 1970, pp. 87–8). The Grotte de Gazel (Sallèles-Cabardès, Aude), whose remarkable stratigraphy has already been mentioned, has a date for one of its earliest Cardial hearths of 4830 ± 200 b.c. and one for a slightly higher hearth of 4590 ± 200 b.c. (Köln dates). The cave of Camprafaud (Ferrières-Poussarou, Hérault) has also produced a remarkable Cardial and Chasséen stratigraphy, and its Cardial Level 19 is dated to 4450 b.c.; the transition Level 17 between the two cultures is dated 4050 b.c. (Rodriguez, 1970).

In the first sequence of dates produced for Châteauneuf-les-Martigues, Hearth 1 was dated 4750 ± 200 b.c. (KN 208); however, in the new sequence, the earliest pottery levels are dated to the fifth millennium (for example, Level 6, 4480 ± 140 b.c. – Ly 446), and Hearth 1 is dated 3960 ± 290 b.c. (Ly 622).

In addition to the series of levels assigned by radiocarbon to the fifth millennium b.c., there are French sites with one level dated to this period such as the rock-shelter of Jean Cros, Labastide-en-Val (Aude) and the open-air site of Le Baratin, Courthézon (Vaucluse).

In order to gain some idea of mid-fifth millennium assemblages, some of the above sites will be described. First, Abri 3 of St Mitre in the upland back-country of Provence, has an assemblage deriving from between two dated layers (4450 and 4750 b.c.). The majority of the assemblage consists of lithic material, principally blades and blade-flakes, and nineteen transverse arrowheads (Calvet, 1969 and Calvet, personal communication).

This site produced a few fragments of querns and several 'jewellery' items, including pierced shells and pierced animal teeth, and a fragment of oval-sectioned pottery bracelet.

The pottery from this level bore various types of decoration, including *Cardium*-impression, deep punctuations and deeply incised lines. Several sherds were decorated with clay pastilles, or vertical cordons, and others bore plastic lugs.

Approximately half the rock-shelter area was excavated (14 m² of about 28 m²), and the analysis of faunal remains indicated the following number of individuals – at least four red deer, one or two roe deer, several boar, one dog, numerous domesticated sheep and eight to ten domesticated cattle. Despite the presence of small wild mammals (for example, beaver, cat), and a bird the main dependence was obviously on the domesticated breeds (Gagnière, in Calvet, 1969, p. 109).

Only a single period of occupation is known from the rock-shelter of Jean Cros, Labastide-en-Val (Aude), located on the edge of a plateau within sight of the sea. The excavator, Guilaine, found a hearth containing *Helix* shells and charcoal under overlying tufas, which has been dated to 4550 ± 300 and 4450 ± 300 b.c. (Guilaine, 1966). The associated assemblage consisted of transverse arrowheads, usually on flakes, and mostly triangular in shape; of twelve illustrated, at least three appear to have been made by the microburin technique (Escalon de Fonton 1970b, fig. 18). There are blades and bladelets, used but rarely retouched, a microlithic segment of a circle, nuclei with two striking platforms and a few objects in rock crystal. This traditional lithic industry was accompanied by a few green-stone axes and thick-walled, probably globular, pottery. Some sherds were undecorated, others bore channelling made by a spatula or bone or stone smoother. Later excavations turned up impressed sherds.

This site is particularly interesting in that Guilaine has been able to distinguish a dispersion of activities in the rock-shelter (Guilaine, 1968). In the southern part are 'heating hearths' – little pits filled with wood charcoal – and a little wall (Guilaine, 1968, fig. 4). Apart from a couple of sherds decorated with either comb or shell impressions, there were few artifacts or faunal remains. However, in the deeper part of the shelter the artifact finds weie richer (transverse arrowheads, bone awls and shell beads) and lay in a dark matrix full of faunal remains and molluscs. Domesticated sheep, goat, cattle, dog and pig have recently been identified by Poulain-Josien (Guilaine, 1971a, p. 118). In addition to this pastoral activity, the occupants of the rock-shelter hunted red and roe deer, boar and marten, and collected hazelnuts and acorns. Several grindstones were found, but there is no more definite indication of agriculture (Guilaine, 1971a, p. 105).

Excavations on the porch of the Grotte de Gazel, an extensive cave on the hilly outskirts of the village of Sallèles-Cabardès (Aude), have recently revealed a continuous stratigraphy of Mesolithic through early, typical and evolved Cardial to Early and Late Chasséen and Chalcolithic (Guilaine, 1970c, pp. 62–4).

Guilaine reports that the final Mesolithic (or proto-Neolithic) Hearth 5 contains backed triangles with a straight or concave retouched base, and a heavy chipped stone component. In the overlying Hearth 4 there is one abruptly retouched transverse arrowhead and a thick flake industry. Pots are not well finished; some of them bear lightly impressed designs, for instance, of vertical parallel lines. Guilaine (1970c, p. 72) reports that the transition to the Neolithic involves the loss of the backed triangle, but that the large chipped stone component remains unchanged. This would seem to argue a certain continuity of tradition in the occupants of the cave as they took over the use of pottery. No information is yet available about structural remains, or faunal evidence, in these two levels.

The Early Neolithic settlers also lit fires inside the cave, where they left pottery decorated by *Cardium* shell and other techniques. Again there is no direct evidence about the economy, but two huge limestone mace-heads or possibly digging-stick weights were found higher up the stratigraphy (Guilaine, 1971a, p. 107).

The cave site of Puechmargues II, La Roque-Ste-Marguerite (Aveyron) also produced pottery in its topmost level, dated $4470 \pm 180$ b.c. (Gif 446). In the same level were marginally retouched triangles and blades, and transverse arrowheads made by the microburin technique (Maury, 1969). Faunal remains are all of wild animals – red deer and roe deer and boar – but a number of grindstones are also known from this site. Pine and oak were used as firewood.

Together with the Grotte de Gazel, which has already been

mentioned, the cave sites of Baume de Montclus and Baume de Fontbrégoua, in the Gard and Var departments respectively, will, when published, produce the fullest record of the systematic changes in raw materials and economy which must have occurred in inland sites over the fifth millennium.

Dates for the Castelnovien levels at Baume de Montclus fall in the mid and late sixth millennium b.c., and the first use of pottery is probably much later than on the coast. Only the Late Cardial ceramics, of the sequence defined at Châteauneuf, appear at Montclus. They are first found in Level 4, which has two radiocarbon dates, of 4450 ± 160 b.c. and 4190 ± 140 b.c. (KN 181 and Ly 303/4).

Excavations by A. Taxil at the Baume de Fontbrégoua revealed Mesolithic occupation under the later Cardial and Chasséen horizons. Courtin has indicated that the Cardial levels have produced wares decorated with *Cardium*, and spatula impressions, and plastic additions. There are rare trapezes (or transverse arrowheads) with abrupt retouch, sickles, and bracelets in polished stone. Carbonized grain was also found in the Cardial levels (Courtin, 1974, p. 35).

The open-air site of Le Baratin, Courthézon (Vaucluse) lies on a low hillside of Miocene sandstone overlooking a valley formerly containing a lake. A trench cut behind a vineyard to prevent storm waters running downhill onto the vines revealed a dense pile of cobbles, associated with potsherds and chipped stone tools. The site has been excavated by Courtin since 1969 and has revealed circular hut floors of cobble-stones (FAH, 1973). Charcoal obtained from the floor of Hut 1 was dated by radiocarbon to 4650 ± 140 b.c. (Courtin, 1972a, p. 118).

Courtin has published illustrations of *Cardium*-decorated ceramics including a handle with multiple holes and *Cardium*-impressed decoration like those in the Gardon valley (Figure 5:1) and emphasized that 99% of all decoration is by this shell (Courtin, 1972a, p. 119). Limestone bracelets of different cross-sections also occur (Courtin, 1968). Flint tools are relatively rare, but include transverse arrowheads with marginal retouch.

The economic strategy at this site must await identification of the animal bones and molluscan remains, and a full pollen analysis.

A little further south down the Rhône valley, excavations at the Quartier de la Balance, Avignon (Vaucluse) have revealed Neolithic occupation over many centuries. A crouched male skeleton with a mass of *Dentalium* and laterally pierced *Columbella* shells and over 3700 small beads cut in marine shell, may date to the Early Neolithic

(Gagnière, 1968, pp. 493–4). The body had been buried in a pit, and an undecorated pointed stela, 40 cm high, stood on the Southern edge of it.

Outside France sites with mid-fifth millennium b.c. radiocarbon dates are fewer in number.

Two dates ($4560 \pm 160$ and $4315 \pm 75$ b.c.) have been obtained on grain samples from a Cardial pottery level at the cave of Coveta de l'Or, located between Alicante and Valencia (Almagro, 1970). The cave is oval, 40 m by 20 m, and stands 650 metres above sea-level. Excavations were conducted in the late 1950s, and are being prepared for publication. The site has produced trapezoidal and semi-lunate microlithic, tanged and barbed arrowheads, geometric arrowheads, small axes, bone awls and spatulae (Schubart and Pascual, 1964). The pottery is impressed with zones of *Cardium*-edge wave-pattern, chevrons, and compositions of vertical and horizontal lines. Deep jars have lugs near the rim. The precise stratigraphic details of the rich material at present housed in the Museo de Prehistoria de la Diputación de Valencia will be of enormous importance. Maria Hopf has identified the grains, in two samples, the richest of which contained a majority of Emmer, followed by naked barley, with a smaller quantity of bread wheat and a few grains of einkorn (Hopf, 1964).

Pending publication of Coveta de l'Or, some indication of the type of assemblage known from sites with *Cardial*-impressed pottery in the Valencia region can be obtained from a study of the material excavated some time ago from the nearby cave of La Sarsa (Valencia) (San Valero, 1950).

The excavations at La Sarsa did not produce a stratigraphy, but shell-fish and carbonized wheat were found in the cave. Bone work seems to have been carefully carried out; long-bones scored for cutting appear among the La Sarsa material, and a number of bone finger-rings, about 1 cm deep by 1–1·5 cm in diameter, have scored decoration around their margins. Awls with serrated handles and bone spoons from the site are illustrated by Tarradell (1962, p. 49). Zigzag and hatched triangle incision appear on other teeth and bones. Together with the rectangular-sectioned slate bracelets, these decorations seem to indicate quite a high degree of personal adornment.

There are also two mid-fifth millennium b.c. dates for Level XVII of the shelter of Araguina-Sennola by the straits of Bonifacio, Corsica, $4480 \pm 140$ b.c. and $4700 \pm 140$ b.c. (Gif 2324,5). The earlier date actually comes from slightly higher up the stratigraphy than the later, but the difference is said to be statistically insignificant (Lanfranchi and Weiss, 1972, p. 383). These Early Neolithic layers contain an interesting series of structures. The three hearths of Level XVIIc overlie a burial, itself cut into by an oval pit. A further hearth is in the lowest level, XVIIe. The material associated with the hearths is also of interest – minute fragments of (snail) shell in Hearth I; shell-fish remains, bones of the hare *Prolagus* and other fauna, and also sherds and lithic fragments.

The skeleton was extended but the lower body had been cut away by the pit. The head was turned to the left, and the arms flexed. The individual was 65–70 years old, male, and fairly small (Engel *in* Lanfranchi and Weiss, 1972, p. 388). Possibly in association was a small round-based vase full of a reddish sandy substance, which stood on a little rock overhang nearby.

The assemblage from Level XVII has not been quantified, but consists of an industry using flint more often than obsidian, flakes more often than blades, and producing trapezoidal and triangular transverse arrowheads. In the pottery punched decoration is the most frequent, and is sometimes associated with straight cordons or big, pierced lugs (Lanfranchi and Weiss, 1972, fig. 6·1). There are rare *Cardium* impressions, and fine incised channels. Only one bone point was found. The absence of ground stone is also unusual.

The economy of this Early Neolithic group was based on shell-fish (oysters, limpets and winkles), fish, *Prolagus,* and wild boar, and possibly some animal raising. Around the strait of Bonifacio a number of other sites were excavated in the last century, similarly with a considerable number of molluscs accompanying the assemblages, both cave and open-air sites. Gagnière, *et al* refer to them as 'kitchen-middens', and record that some of them produced obsidian, pottery and pierced *Columbella* shells (Gagnière, *et al*, 1969, p. 388).

By the fifth millennium b.c. many sites on the Italian mainland had pottery, although we still have no confirmatory dates from the Po valley area.

At the Romagnano III site in the Adige valley, mentioned in the last chapter, the Tardenoid without pottery is succeeded in Levels AA1–2 by a Tardenoid industry with pottery. Recognizably Fiorano pottery appears in the overlying Levels T3–4; Fiorano Ware is the first clearly defined ceramic stage in North-East Italy (Barfield, 1971, p. 36), and is represented at eleven sites in the Eastern Po valley and the surrounding hills.

Broglio contrasts the mainly rock-shelter occupation of the valley bottom practised in the pre-pottery sites with the occupation of some open sites in the Fiorano phase (Broglio, 1973, p. 159). This culture should presumably be dated in the late fifth millennium b.c. (the date for Chiozza di Scandiano is 4050 ± 200 b.c.). Fiorano pottery is well-made in open bowl, deep carinated and bucket shapes (Barfield, 1971, fig. 14), the first two types decorated with incised chevrons and ring handles with little bosses (Figures 7:1–3). The traditional lithic industry has already been mentioned, and hunting continued; however, domesticated plants and animals are evidenced on Fiorano sites (for example, barley at Chiozza – Bagolini and Barfield, 1970). Barfield maintains that the frequent pits found on Fiorano and other Italian sites were for storage of grain or other produce, no doubt after the clay contents had been used for the walls of real huts (Barfield, 1971, p. 38).

Although the first pottery in Northern Italy belongs to the Fiorano culture, the Ligurian coast is firmly in the main West Mediterranean mainstream. Impressed Ware appears in the lower levels of the stratified Arene Candide cave (Bernabò Brea, 1946; 1956), and in other Ligurian cave assemblages. Level 25 at Arene Candide has been dated 4614 ± 135 b.c. It contains two bone awls, and a double point (presumably for fishing) and occasionally bones or shells are pierced for use, perhaps as pendants. No obsidian is indicated from this level – and only seven flint tools or nuclei – but an obsidian flake is known from the earlier Level 26 (Bernabò Brea, 1956, tav. XI, 4b). There is a single steatite cylinder. The potsherds illustrated are well decorated by impression or, very rarely, deep cuts and punches. Brea indicates that a majority of the impressions are always by *Cardium* shell, and in fact a number probably bear *Petonculus* shell impressions or those made by animal bone splinters or teeth (Bernabò Brea, 1956, p. 59). Brea feels that the decoration probably covered the whole surface of the deep bowls and jars. Near lugs and handles the impressions often approach at an angle to each other (for example, Bernabò Brea, 1956, plate IX, 1.3,7). Other decorative motifs include cordons, usually with punched impression. Rare pottery spoons and a minute axe were found in surrounding levels.

As a result of studies published by Emiliani, *et al* (1964) it has been established that a majority of the faunal remains in the Early Neolithic levels were of domesticated species, but that remains of wild animals including red deer indicated 'an appreciable hunting activity' (Emiliani, *et al*, 1964, p. 136). According to figure 2 of this report, Levels 25–6 contained, amongst the domesticated species, a predominance of sheep, followed by pig, with very small complement of goat and even less cattle.

There are no proofs of domesticated grains in Level 25 but Evett and Renfrew have identified Emmer and barley in the overlying Level 22 (Evett and Renfrew, 1971, p. 409).

In Central and Southern Italy the Neolithic occupation of the fifth millennium is less clearly defined. There are elements of the Fiorano culture at Ripabianca, a site on the very South-Eastern edge of the Po plain near the coastal town of Ancona. The Ancona area is also the Northernmost limit of the Impressed Ware pottery which is an important element of Southern Italian Neolithic cultures until after 4000 b.c. Italian and British writers (Stevenson, 1947; Bernabò Brea, 1957; Trump, 1966; Peroni, 1967) have argued until recently that the Early Neolithic consisted of purely Impressed Ware groups, and was an extremely short period. Whitehouse has suggested, from the extreme rarity of sites without any painted ware, that in fact there is no cultural or other break in the Early Neolithic, and that Red-painted Wares were present, albeit in small quantities, from the very earliest Neolithic occupation (Whitehouse, 1969, p. 272). For instance, the Capo d'Acqua site mentioned in the last chapter produced Impressed and Red-painted Wares (Bonuccelli and Faedo, 1968, p. 100). Brea's excavations at Lipari (Sicily) in a sense confirm this priority, since in his lowest stratum Impressed, Red-painted and Matera-type scratched Wares were found together (Bernabò Brea and Cavalier, 1960). The Matera scratched Ware is one of many local variants that sprang up in the general ambit of Impressed and Red-painted cultures (Whitehouse, 1969, p. 298). Trichrome Wares (usually red and black on buff) are generally regarded as a later development.

The site of Scaramella, dated by radiocarbon to the early and mid-fifth millennium b.c., is the most recently excavated of the numerous ditched sites of the Tavoliere plain (Stevenson, 1947). These sites, as is well known, were discovered by aerial photography towards the end of World War II; some 230 sites are visible on aerial photographs,

*Figure 4. Monte Aquilone, Manfredonia (Apulia). No. 1, Ditched settlement in plan; No. 2, Walled house revealed at W inside innermost ditch; Nos. 3, 4, sherds of bowls with respectively impressed and incised-plus-painted decoration (after Manfredini).*

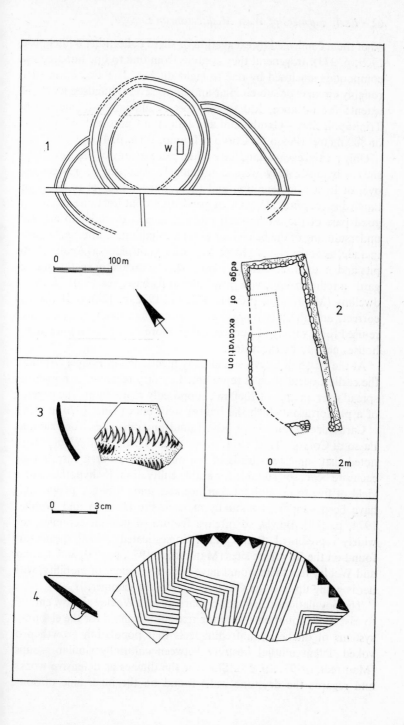

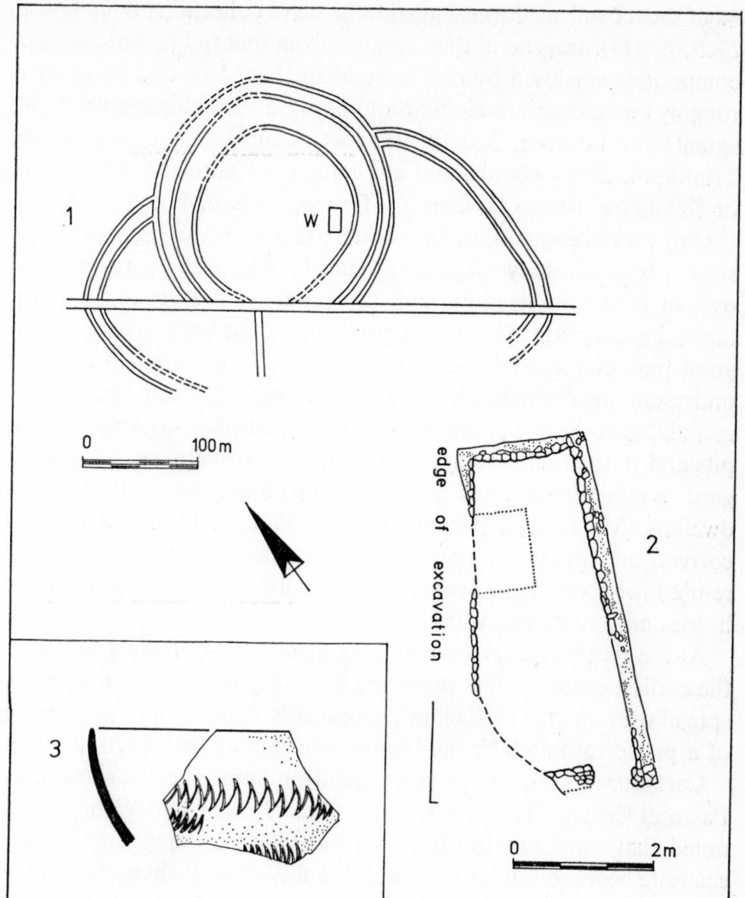
1
W
0
100 m
2
edge of excavation
0
2 m
3
0
3 cm
4

40 of them confirmed by excavation or sherd collection (Whitehouse, 1969, p. 273). In general they contain from one to one hundred hut compounds, enclosed by one to eight ditches. The area enclosed is roughly circular or sub-circular and up to several hundred metres in extent; for instance, 220 to 300 metres maximum diameter (the Trinitapoli sites – Gambassini and Palma di Cesnola, 1967, p. 335), or 800 metres (Passo Di Corvo – Trump, 1966, p. 41).

Only partial excavations have taken place on any of these extensive sites; obviously they were continuously occupied or re-occupied over at least a millennium, and this sequence has yet to be disentangled successfully. Open area excavation of at least one site over a good part of the ditches and internal area is essential to any full understanding of the behaviour of their inhabitants. Internal features include, as at the site of Monte Aquilone, Manfredonia (Apulia), both pits and house foundations (Figure 4). The excavator of this site regards an elliptical pit, with post-holes at its base, as an early form of dwelling (Manfredini, 1969, p. 375, and 1972, p. 128). If Barfield is correct, and the pits represent no more than daub quarries, later re-used for a variety of purposes, then more of the stone foundation houses need to be excavated.

At the Passo di Corvo site already mentioned in Foggia (Apulia), the earliest occupation is represented by fifty rectangular post-holes spread over an area of 7000 m², supposedly representing the pegging of a platform on which the houses were built (Tine, 1970, p. 428).

Carbonized grains have been found on some sites (for example, Passo di Corvo – Tine, 1971, p. 488), and Jarman and Webley have noted that some two-thirds of the one-kilometre area surrounding each site bears soil suitable for arable cultivation. By hypothesizing a yield of five to ten quintals per hectare, some fifty-five people may have been supported annually at each site (Jarman and Webley, 1974, p. 189). Bowls, so often a feature of peasant ceramics, are widely represented. Bones of all domesticated animal species are found on the Tavoliere sites (Manfredini, 1972, p. 153), and Jarman and Webley feel there would have been an element of mobility, with herds going up into the Gargano hills in the summer.

The populations calculated by Jarman and Webley are low enough to cast some doubt on one of the reasons advanced for the elaborate systems of ditches. Manfredini feels that population growth provoked 'latent mutual hostility between culturally similar groups' (Manfredini, 1972, p. 55). She sees the ditches as defensive works, and regards the drystone walls found on the inner side of some ditches as supporting evidence. No offensive weapons – arrowheads, for instance – have ever been found. Other explanations for the ditches is that they were used for drainage (Tine) or to control livestock (Whitehouse).

Soundings have recently been made in eight ditched Neolithic villages detected by air photography at San Vito on the Tavoliere plain to the South-East of Foggia. The Scaramella village has two dates on charcoal from the bottom of two concentric circular ditches surrounding the site, 5050 ± 100 b.c. for Scaramella A–I and 4590 ± 65 b.c. for Scaramella A–II (R350 and R351). The accompanying pottery is either impressed or painted in red or black geometric designs on the buff surface (Alessio and Bella, 1969, p. 486). The ditched villages, together with the monochrome painted pottery, thus seem to have been present in Southern Italy since the earliest Neolithic.

Other open-air sites with similar dates are the Leopardi village in Abruzzo and the Maddalena di Muccia and Ripabianca di Monterado sites in Marche; all have so-called 'pit dwellings'.

The Leopardi site, 4614 ± 135 b.c. (Pisa) and 4228 ± 135 b.c. (Pi 101) consisted of three ellipsoid pits approximately four metres long by three metres wide (Cremonesi, 1966). Nearly a thousand fragments of baked clay bearing imprints of beams and sticks represent walling. The lithic industry was of mainly unretouched flakes and some blades, but included a burin, a truncation and a sickle blade. There was no obsidian present. A few impressed sherds (2% of the total ceramics) bore finger-nail impressions which seemed to cover most of the bowls down to the footed base. Most of the pottery, however, was well-made of either reddish or dark fabrics, and consisted of flat or footed-base deep jars or hemispherical bowls; some of the dark bowls had a high carination. There were thicker-walled jars in two different fabrics and *figulina* (fine yellowish ware) was represented by five sherds with reddish-violet painting inside.

The normal domesticated species are represented at Leopardi (Barker, 1974b), and Evett and Renfrew have indicated the presence of a few grains of barley and Emmer (Evett and Renfrew, 1971, p. 409).

The site of Maddalena di Muccia lies on a fluvial terrace between two rivers, and consists of multiple pits dug to different depths, full of potsherds and lithic material; only a short preliminary report has appeared (Lollini, 1965). The site is dated 4630 ± 75 b.c. (R 643a), and the industry consists of both Mesolithic-derived flint (pointed blades, transverse arrowheads and rhombs, burins) and a little imported obsidian; there are also a few fragments of quern, but no signs of grain. The flat-based pottery is both impressed and wet-incised, using fingers, nails, bone points, pinching and so on, in all-over patterns. A rather better-made ware is smoothed and decorated with lugs. The shapes are flask, jar and carinated. Apparently sheep and goat were herded at the site (Barker, 1974b, p. 133) but boar and red deer are also represented.

Dr Lollini has also excavated the site of <u>Ripabianca di Monterado</u> on the right bank of the Cesaro river. This site has just one pit, more than 8 metres long, and 1·50 metres deep at its deepest point. Daub marked with branch indentations presumably represents hut walling. This site has four radiocarbon dates ranging from $4310 \pm 85$ b.c. to $4190 \pm 70$ b.c. (R599a, R598a). The pottery from the site includes the finger and point impressed decoration found at Maddalena di Muccia, both all over the pot and in neat zones. There is a fragment of red-painted *figulina* ware and two female idols in clay. The blade industry is rather less regular than at Maddalena, with frequent truncations, and a few querns are known from the site.

The notable ceramic traits in Central Italy in the fifth millennium b.c. are thus impressed designs, not usually carried out using shells, and painted pottery. In Ruth Whitehouse's view the 'pure' Impressed Ware sites do not occupy a separate horizon in Southern and Central Italy, and were occupied by acculturated Mesolithic peoples (Whitehouse, 1969, p. 272).

Even in the area of West Mediterranean Europe most addicted to shell impression (from Liguria to Eastern Spain), there is a change of technique over time. In an article giving some of the radiocarbon dates, Guilaine and Calvet indicate the pottery decorative attributes found at the different periods (Guilaine and Calvet, 1970). Hearth 4 at Grotte de Gazel (Aude), with the earliest carbon-14 date, has associated *Cardium*-impressed pottery, whereas pottery from Hearth 1, with a more recent date, rarely bears *Cardium* impression, being decorated instead with vertical or horizontal chevron, zig-zag or obliquely stroked designs (made presumably with a bone or stone or wooden implement). The surface of other sherds is roughened by channels crossing each other, or by the presence of smooth or slightly indented cordons.

In France the reduction of decoration by *Cardium* shell is fairly standard (though there are regional differences); it occurs at the

*Cardium*-impressed pottery from Montserrat caves

Camprafaud cave (Hérault) and rock-shelter 3 of St Mitre (Basses-Alpes). At Camprafaud Level 19, dated to 4450 b.c., there are bands and flames and garlands impressed in *Cardium* technique, but the succeeding Levels 18 and 17 have no shell impression, only punctuate decoration; Level 17 is dated 4050 b.c. (Rodriguez, 1970). The mid-fifth millennium b.c. horizon at Abri 3 de St Mitre has already been described; from being present on about a third of the sherds, *Cardium* decoration falls off in the overlying level to a single sherd (Calvet, 1969, p. 76).

A similar phenomenon is visible at Châteauneuf-les-Martigues. The proportion of *Cardium*-impressed sherds to the total number of sherds recovered goes down from less than a half in Level 6 to approximately a third in Hearth 5 and Hearth 4. They constitute about an eighth of the whole in Level 2, and have nearly disappeared by Hearth 1.

In contrast to this reduction in *Cardium* impression, channelling and punctuate ornament increase over time. Channelling begins in the mid-fifth millennium (Gazel, Camprafaud). The Late Cardial at Grotte de Gazel (Levels 2a–2c – not dated) contains sherds with furrow or dot designs and impressed cordons (Guilaine, 1970b, p. 165). Only punctuate ornament is present in Level 17 (4050 b.c.) at Camprafaud. The same elements begin at Châteauneuf in Level 2. It would be wrong to be too dogmatic about the temporal value of any of these features, however, because they seem to vary regionally. ✱ For instance, *Cardium* impression seems to vanish very early in South-Western France (Gazel) but remains in vogue in Provence (Courtin, 1972a, p. 119). There are also regional emphases – 'grape' clusters of fat paste lumps are particularly popular in the Gardon valley, Vaucluse, Basses-Alpes, and up to Le Puy.

Combinations of vertical and horizontal cordons commence in Hearth 5 at Châteauneuf-les-Martigues, and in Level 2c of the Grotte de Gazel cave stratigraphy (Guilaine, 1970c, p. 70). This particular design seems to have been a very popular type, and also appears frequently in the Gardon valley (Fig. 5).

The pottery in Level C at Roucadour (Lot), dated $3900 \pm 150$ b.c. (GsY 36a) was decorated with buttons and cordons, while a number of sherds also bore stamped or nail-impressed designs or horizontal channelling. The date was obtained from grain found in the level, so presumably farming was practised, although the faunal remains were nearly completely of wild species (Niederlender, Arnal and Lacam, 1966, pp. 29–31).

E

This change over time in pottery decoration techniques *may* be linked to the presumably greater problems of obtaining sea-shells as the habit of pottery-making was adopted by successively more inland peoples.

A cross-cutting development to the reduction of shell impressions on pottery in the Cardial period is the development of regional emphases or pottery attribute clusters ('types'). Two particular examples of this can be given – the pottery of the Gardon valley, Central Southern France, and the pottery of Eastern Spain.

The river Gardon lies in the Gard department to the West of the Rhône. Most of the caves in its limestone cliffs were excavated in the last century. Much of the material has been lost, and there is no proof of Mesolithic occupation. However, some of the ceramic finds are preserved in the museums of Nîmes and Montpellier, and show the rich variety of impressed and plastic designs used on the Cardial ware (Figure 5).

The St Vérédème cave has produced a large number of *Cardium*-impressed sherds, including sherds of deep bowls decorated with horizontal and vertical bands of shell impression, each band delimited by a long line of edging. *Cardium* impressions also run in bands towards huge tri-pierced handles, the backs of which are also decorated by impression; a little impressed clay button lies at the base of each handle (for example, Figure 5:1). St Vérédème is also rich in plastic ornamented wares, like the enormous thick-walled jar shown in Figure 5:3. This jar bears a triangular-sectioned internal cordon below the rim, while its outer wall is decorated alternately with vertical plastic cordons and rows of fat pastilles, both spilling over the rim. Less elaborate cordons decorate jars from Baume Latrone and Grotte Féraud. Both of these caves have produced examples of the 'bunch of grapes' design, in which a central set of plastic buttons is surrounded by a cordon, from which other cordons stretch out in a star-like design (Figure 5:2).

Similar impressed and plastic design elements appear in material from other Gardon valley caves (Pâques, Sartanette, Seynes, Figuier and Mazauric caves), confirming the regional styles of the area. There may even be a certain continuity of tradition in the Gardon

*Figure 5. Early Neolithic pottery of Gardon valley. Nos. 1 and 3, St Vérédème cave; Nos. 2 and 4, Féraud cave; No. 5, Baume Latrone. Scale – one-quarter natural size.*

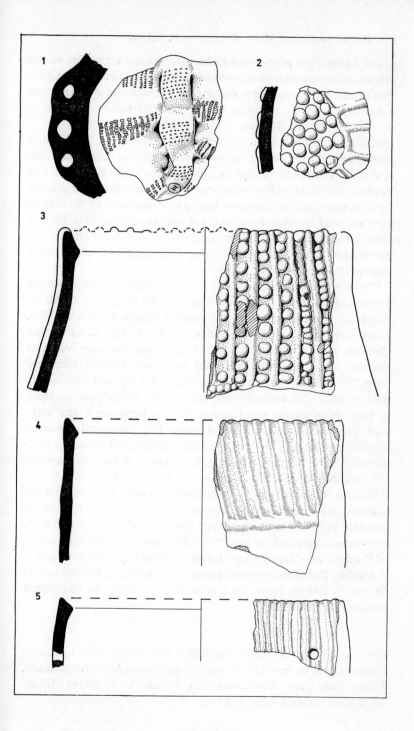

valley, because the edge-zoned *Cardium*-impressed areas may be the precursors of the edge-zoned cross-hatched areas decorating Chasséen vessels in the same area, and the same location of the ornament – slightly below the rim and on the outside of the vessels – persists in the Gardon valley Chasséen.

The same phenomenon of regionalism visible in the Cardial pottery of Southern France has long been evident in the publications of Spanish Cardial ware. *Cardium* impressions in the Barcelona and Valencia areas (the two zones nearest to the Pyrenees) have distinct features, especially as regards using the proximal nose of the shell to form an oval serrated zone, some 4 mm in length. This zone is usually added as a pendant to vertical or oblique lines of impression. But the two regions have in addition distinct features which mark them off from each other.

The Barcelona Neolithic has been most widely known since the publications of finds from the caves near the monastery of Montserrat, sixty kilometres from the coast (Colomines i Roca, 1925). Finds were made principally in Cova Gran and Cova Freda, Collbato. No stratigraphy was noted, but of the obviously Neolithic material, there are both impressed vases and smooth burnished ware. The most significant elements here for a regional division are the handles – both vertically and horizontally pierced, and reaching in both cases to the rim (Figures 6:1, 2). Both small and large vertically pierced handles are known. The horizontally pierced handles are thinner, more of the strap variety, and form a continuous line with the pot wall. In at least one case there is a typical button appendix on the base of the handle.

Oblique, horizontal and vertical lines of impression surround the handles, and in many cases decorate them as well. In one case an alternate form of decoration, very shallow horizontal channelling, covers the handle and the lower part of the pot wall – following a row of *Cardium* 'nose' impressions, the channelling is arranged vertically.

Another *Cardium*-impressed example of a vertically pierced handle on rim is known from the Cueva Bonica, Vallirona (Barcelona Museum) (Figure 6:4).

---

*Figure 6. Barcelona Early Neolithic. Rim sherds with* Cardium-*impression and horizontally or vertically perforated lugs on rim. Nos. 1, 2 from Cova Gran, Montserrat; No. 3 from Toll de Moya, Moya; No. 4 from Cueva Bonica, Vallirona. Scale – half natural size.*

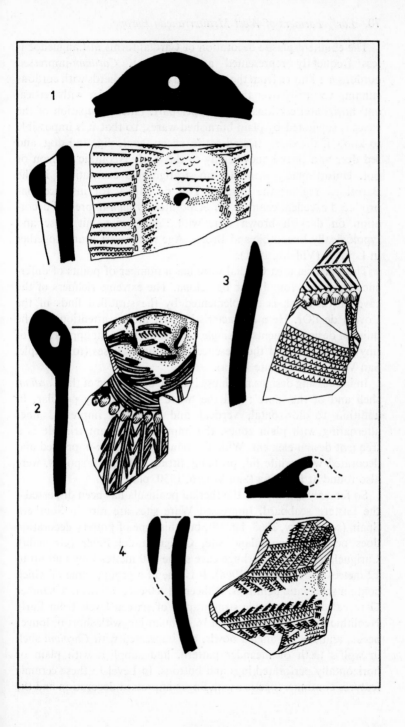

The ebullient plastic decoration of Cardial forms in Languedoc is less frequently represented at Montserrat. *Cardium*-impressed cordons are known from the caves, and there are sherds with cordons running vertically over the rim, and an enormous jar with vertical and horizontal cordons on its upper part. Later occupation of the caves is suggested by plain burnished wares, so that it is impossible to know if the domesticated cattle, sheep, goat, pig, and dog, and red deer and boar bones belong to the Early Neolithic horizon or not. Unfortunately there are no stratigraphic excavations in the Barcelona region; the cave of Toll de Moya, for instance, has produced excellent examples of elaborate *Cardium*-impressed decoration on darkish brown ware with sandy grits, but these and typologically Eneolithic and Bronze Age wares were found together in Level A (Villalta, 1971).

The Valencia area Cardial ware has a number of points of difference from that found near Barcelona. The extreme richness of the cave of La Sarsa is complemented by the stratified finds of the Coveta de l'Or. Here characteristics that attract attention are the unity of design elements on single vessels, the frequent appearance of tiny 'toy' vases, and the presence of 'twinned' vases (for example, San Valero, 1950, plate XIVa).

In impressing designs much use is made of the edge of the *Cardium* shell and of the 'nose'; and the 'wave' motif is very popular. In addition to horizontal, vertical and obliquely impressed lines alternating with plain zones, the impressed pendant triangle is a frequent design element. Wide flat handles, *Cardium*-impressed and decorated with white fill, probably fitting onto huge spoons, were also found at La Sarsa (San Valero, 1950, plate 8.3).

So far only one area of the Iberian peninsula has been discussed – the Eastern seaboard. Impressed Ware sites are rare in Southern Spain (*see* Savory, 1968, fig. 18), but this type of pottery decoration does occur in one inland site, Cariguela del Piñar (Granada). Cariguela del Piñar is a huge cave some 300 metres long and up to 12 metres wide (Pellicer, 1964). It is one of a group, some of which contain schematic paintings. Pellicer's 1960 excavations in Chamber G revealed a remarkable stratigraphy of sixteen levels from Early Neolithic to Bronze II. In Level 16 globular jars with short or longer necks, and steeply angled bowls, are impressed with *Cardium* shell in wolf's teeth or meander pattern, and supplied with plain or horizontally perforated lugs and buttons. In Level 15 these ceramic features continue, together with finger-impressed decoration and the presence of red-slipped ware (*a la almagra*). Red-slipped ware is widely known in the Spanish Neolithic and Copper Ages, and its date has been much argued. Pellicer regarded it as Middle Neolithic (Pellicer, 1964, p. 57). However, as will be shown below, there is a good reason for believing that such pottery was being produced in the late fifth millennium b.c., and the Cariguela occupation may well begin at that time. The impressed and red-slipped wares continue in use up to Level 10. Serpentine bracelets first occur in Level 14, and limestone ones in the succeeding Level 13.

Unfortunately we do not have much idea of the economy of the Cariguela occupants, although Savory mentions that grain was recovered (Savory, 1968, p. 76); certainly querns are found from Level 13 onwards, many of them stained with ochre, as though used for colourant rather than food grinding. Faunal remains for the different levels have not been quantified.

Red-slipped pottery has been decisively dated by twelve radio-carbon dates on grain and wood running from $4300 \pm 35$ to $3980 \pm 130$ b.c., coming from three Neolithic levels of Cueva Chica, part of the Los Murciélagos cave complex, near Zuheros, Cordoba (Vicent and Muñoz, 1973). The grain, which is to be published by Dr Maria Hopf, had been stored in a pit; acorns were also consumed at the site, and the bones of domesticated sheep, goat, cattle and pig have been identified (Vicent and Muñoz, 1973, pp. 98–104). The pit also contained red-slipped pottery, which is present in all three Neolithic levels of the site. It comes in a variety of deep bowls with incised designs and paired handles, the latter sometimes incorporated in vertical cordons. A toothed bone tool found in Level IV may have incised some of the designs. Stone bracelets are present, as at Cariguela; there are two varieties, a plain plump type and a wide thin type incised with one to four red-filled concentric rings. The red colourant may have been ochre: a stone mortar stained with this mineral was found in Level IV, and lumps of ochre in the assemblage suggest that considerable use was made of it.

Although generally not practised around the Southern Spanish seaboard, the habit of impressing *Cardium* shells on pottery did reach Portugal. The ceramic finds have recently been discussed by Guilaine and da Veiga (1970), who find that most of the known sites cluster near the coast or on rivers in Central Portugal (Cabo Mondego). They feel that a date in the early fifth millennium can be assigned to the early, much-impressed sherds. The impressions often lie in rows of short vertical indents, below rims decorated with plain or pierced buttons. There is apparently no use of the 'nose' or pendant triangle motifs so beloved of the East coast Iberians. The only cultural associations mentioned are of many axes found with *Cardium*-impressed sherds at the Sagres Point (Southern Portugal), and of marginally retouched transverse arrowheads formed by the micro-burin technique with impressed sherds at the Grotte d' Escoural. The Tagus shell-middens, which must have been occupied at much the same time, have not produced *Cardium*-impressed ware.

In Portugal as in the East of the Iberian peninsula, this stylistic fashion does not seem to have been replaced until perhaps the beginning of the third millennium, some time after the introduction of the first megalithic structures.

Thus the Iberian peninsula, very much like the French land-mass, seems to have been the scene of numerous localized systematic changes during the critical fifth millennium b.c. The use of pottery in at least one site (Coveta de l'Or) seems to be linked with grain storage, but even at this site the other domesticated standbys are unknown. Portugal presents a picture of firmly sea- and fresh-water orientated economies, with the Tagus valley shell-middens apparently unaffected by Neolithic traits, and some lagoon-side settlement, for instance at Possanco near Comporta, which will be discussed in the next chapter.

There are still no definite Mesolithic sites known in Sardinia (Lilliu, 1972, p. 21), but impressed vases from a number of sites now support the hypothesis of an Early Neolithic occupation. A biconical jar, with impressed decoration on neck and handle, was found in the Grotta Rifugio, Oliena (Nuoro) (Carta, 1966–7), together with five bracelets of the shell *Triton*. More recently pottery decorated with bands of shell-impressed lines has been found at the Grotta dell'Inferno, Muros (Sassari) (Contu, 1970, p. 435 and Sassari Museum display). Dr David Trump will be excavating at Grotta dell'Inferno and hopefully a much larger sample of stratified Early Neolithic material will emerge. The rock-shelter excavated by Lilliu at Cala di Vela Marina on the archipelago of La Maddalena in North-Eastern Sardinia produced sherds from one carinated and one plain bowl, and a sherd with a row of oblong impressed dots (illustrated by Guido, 1963, fig. 11). Lilliu reported that the sherds were all convex-walled, and there seemed to be no flat-based bowls; also, the pottery had probably been made locally, using quartz and mica grits. The lithic industry of 200 pieces used 71% imported obsidian, 14% quartz, 8·5% granite and 6·5% porphyry, all three latter materials locally available. He hypothesized that the industry, although archaic in possessing microliths (notably one lunate, Lilliu, 1959, fig. VII.10), probably was nearer in date to the middle levels at Arene Candide (*bocca quadrata* phase) than the earlier. A few mammal bones (notably of the large hare *Prolagus*), and a few bird and fish bones were found; but the subsistence of the small group who inhabited Cala di Vela Marina was obviously largely based on marine and terrestrial molluscs. Many shells of *Patella ferruginea* were found.

The economy of the other Early Neolithic settlers in Sardinia is not known; no food remains are reported from Grotta Rifugio, and stratified excavations remain to be carried out at Grotta dell'Inferno.

Towards the end of the Early Neolithic a number of caves and open-air sites were occupied for the first time, or at least for the first time since the end of the Würm glaciation. The Middle Gorges of the Verdon River have provided examples of this phenomenon. The only site with a complete Cardial assemblage is the river-side rock-shelter called Abri du Jardin du Capitaine, Ste-Croix-du-Verdon (Basses-Alpes). The Cardial level has been dated $4100 \pm 150$ b.c. (Gif 1111). The pottery is round-based with a few *Cardium* impressions; stone implements include transverse arrowheads with marginal retouch, a burin, steeply retouched flakes and flake-blades, 'choppers' (river cobbles with a few flakes struck off them) and a quern. Cobbles were used for making a hearth. There are cattle, sheep and fish bones, and mollusc shells (Gagnière, 1968, pp. 508–9). The Abri du Jardin du Capitaine continued to be occupied during the succeeding millennium b.c., together with other caves in the same gorges.

It can thus be seen that the first 1500 years of the new living style in West Mediterranean Europe produced great variety in economic practice. Molluscs still formed a staple element of the diet at Coppa Nevigata, Cap Ragnon and Île Riou in the mid-sixth millennium, and rather later at the Jean Cros cave and on Corsica and Sardinia. Elsewhere sheep were widely herded, sometimes in association with wild species, but more often with other domesticated species. Grain is definitely being cultivated by the mid-fifth millennium in Spain and Southern France, and probably also in Italy.

Despite the continuity of the chipped stone tools and the use of ochre, new elements creep in with the development of the grinding technique. Stone bracelets are found in Sardinia, France and Spain, and bone finger-rings in Eastern Spain. During this period decoration of the living, and care of the dead, seem to become more important. Shells, animal teeth and animal bones are pierced more frequently than in the Mesolithic, and are found in occupation levels and with burials. These various jewellery items may indicate increased need for personal identification of the individual. The role of the individual is becoming more important, although in most parts of West Mediterranean Europe he is still one of a smallish group with regional ties.

By 4000 b.c. a few daring traders are crossing stretches of the inland sea and moving goods between islands and the continent. So far we can only detect a few elements of this trade, particularly the obsidian, but it means the beginning of more intensive communication between the West Mediterranean communities.

# 4. The Fourth Millennium b.c.

Slowly, piecemeal, farming techniques creep across West Mediterranean Europe. From the surviving evidence, the communities of the fourth millennium b.c. seem to have been industrious and technically adept – the pottery they produce is often fine-walled, highly burnished and elegantly decorated in incised or painted designs. In Southern France the manufacture of pottery seems to have been a local, probably familial task; the same may be true of most areas of West Mediterranean Europe, perhaps with the exception of Southern Italy. There was regional specialization, but general homogeneity of material culture pervaded wide areas. The fourth millennium societies seem to have been open to trade and cross-cultural influences and it is difficult to detect warlike activities. The overriding impression is of fairly small populations, from a dozen to under a hundred persons commonly residing together, intent upon an increasingly domesticate-based economy, in a situation where land hunger was still not a problem, and where the primeval forest provided firewood, grazing and game.

More open-air sites are added to the traditional cave and rock-shelter dwellings, and a slow population build-up commences in favoured areas, foreshadowing the large and elaborate settlements of the next millennium. In the latter half of the period some societies in Portugal, Italy and Malta begin to bury their dead in megalithic tombs and rock-cut sepulchres, a cult that was to grow to massive proportions later.

We know nothing of the struggles to push back the forest, the taming of local animal populations and the way in which control of stocks and land was vested in the new farming societies. Doubtless ancestor spirits or supernatural bodies were credited with some hand in the fertility of crops and livestock. The sun motif on pottery and cave walls, the rare figurines, and rock art in Northern Italy, South-East France and Spain are our only reminders of these beliefs.

Perhaps around the turn of the fourth millennium b.c., perhaps several hundred years before, the Western Po valley area saw the development of a culture using square-mouthed pottery, which spread later over the area occupied by the Fiorano culture. Barfield has recently excavated a site belonging to an early phase of this culture at Molino Casarotto near Vicenza (Veneto); here timber platforms supporting three large hearths were erected on an earlier lake shore (Bagolini, Barfield and Broglio, 1973, fig. 2). The economy of the site was based on collecting and hunting; the lake supplied mussel, pike and turtle and water chestnuts, and the slopes of the Berici hills, red deer and boar. There are small quantities of domesticated sheep and cattle bones, and water sieving revealed a few carbonized grains of wheat and grape pips (Jarman, 1971, p. 263; 1972, p. 136).

The lithic industry of Molino Casarotto does not owe much to the Mesolithic tradition – blades are the basis for tanged arrowheads, end-scrapers, burins and awls, and flat retouch is common. Wear pattern analysis reveals that three end-scrapers were used respectively for polishing, rubbing and cutting (Bagolini, Barfield and Broglio, 1973, figs. 28–9). Ground stone manufactures include axes and chisels and bracelets. The fine pottery is flat-based for the most part and comprises wide bowls, square-necked jars, and pedestal and round-based vases with square mouths (Barfield, 1971, plates 13, 14). Incised decoration in geometric designs covers these wares. Clay *'pintaderas'* or stamps are also known from the site, and human teeth and rabbit metatarsals were bored for suspension (Bagolini, Barfield and Broglio, 1973, fig. 33.1–7).

Molino Casarotto has two series of radiocarbon dates – the first run from $4520 \pm 150$ to $4175 \pm 150$ b.c. (Birm. 176, 177), the second – which the excavator prefers – from $3800 \pm 150$ to $3500 \pm 150$ b.c. (Birm. 262, 266).

Further West in the Po valley is the remarkable site of Isola Virginia, an island in Lake Varese (Lombardy). A series of excavations have taken place at the site since the middle of the last century (Castelfranco, 1916), and the most recent excavations by Bertelone are being prepared for publication by Fusco and Guerreschi (preliminary report, 1966). The site consisted of a lakeside village built on piles and a wooden platform. The platform has two radiocarbon dates ($3584 \pm 144$ and $3376 \pm 180$ b.c. – Pi-4 and Pi-38). The material lying immediately above this platform belongs to the Square-Mouthed Pottery culture (Rivoli-Spiazzo phase as defined by Barfield). Daub was found, and some pot bases bear impressions of

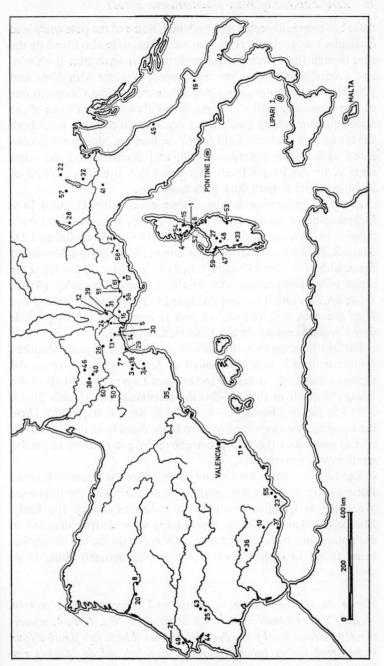

*Map 4 (see p. 14)*

what has been interpreted as a rush mat. Some of the pots contained carbonized acorn mush. Hazelnuts and wheat were also found on the site, though their stratigraphic provenance is uncertain. Both wild and domesticated fauna are represented, together with birds and pike. Altogether an economy not unlike the Molino Casarotto one can be suggested. Soffredi has published illustrations of some of the wide square-mouthed bowls from the site, which come from both the lowest and the later, Late Neolithic, horizon. Most were quadrilobed rather than square-mouthed, and decorated on the outer surface. In the lowest levels this decoration usually consisted of incision on the smooth dark brown surfaces.

A recent excavation in the Gaban rock-shelter (Trento) in a Quinzano-phase Square-Mouthed Pottery level produced a female figurine in clay, and a decorated handle in bone (Bagolini and De Marinis, 1973). The latter bears as one of its designs the *'orante'* or figure with raised arms (Figure 7:4). This design is well known at the series of rock-engraving sites in the Valcamonica valley (Anati, 1960; 1963), where it has been assigned to the Neolithic Styles I and II of the rock art. The Gaban find is interesting for its possible chronological bearing on the Valcamonica figures.

Barfield believes that the earliest stage of the Square-Mouthed Pottery culture is also represented at Arene Candide cave on the Ligurian coast. The dates for the relevant Layers 14 to 24 (Bernabò Brea, 1956) fall in the mid-fourth millennium b.c. (Levels 21–24, $3385 \pm 50$ b.c. and Levels 16–19, $3515 \pm 50$ b.c. – R103, R102). There is a considerable amount of overlap in the dates from different levels of this cave, and the two given above do not fit their respective stratigraphic provenances.

The Ligurian caves are the only area where the Square-Mouthed Pottery cultures have a stratigraphic relationship with the Impressed Ware. Arene Candide has been published as though the Early, Middle and Late Neolithic assemblages were sharply opposed to each other, but there are instances of sherds with incised decoration being found in earlier levels (for example, Bernabò Brea, 1956:

---

*Figure 7. Northern Italy. Fiorano and square-mouthed pottery. Nos. 1, 2, 3, Fiorano ware (after Malavolti); Nos. 6, 5, 4, square-mouthed incised bowl from Pescale, decorated bone and figurine from Gaban rock-shelter (after Malavolti, Bagolini and de Marinis respectively).*

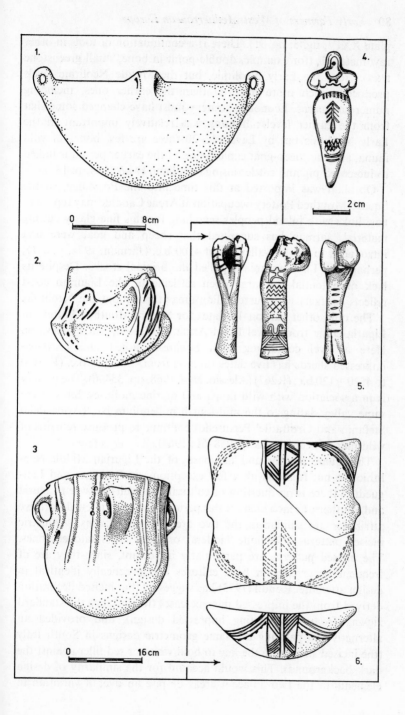

1.

2.

3

4.

2 cm

0        8 cm

5.

0            16 cm

6.

plate XXIV, fig. 5, fig. 9f). There is a continuation of tools in other raw materials (for example, double point in bone, small greenstone axes), from the Early Neolithic, but the Middle Neolithic levels produced much more material than the earlier ones, including numerous querns. Economic strategy must have changed somewhat from the earlier levels; hunting was relatively important in the Early Neolithic but by Levels 17–20 there are few bones of wild fauna, and the sheep-goat exploitation of the earlier period is linked to increased pig and cattle raising (Emiliani, *et al,* 1964, p. 137).

Obsidian was imported at this time into the Po valley, so the Square-Mouthed Pottery occupation at Arene Candide may represent new links with inland peoples searching for this fine glassy cutting material. Jarman has suggested that sheep and goat were first introduced to the Po valley about 4500 b.c. (Jarman, 1971, p. 261); perhaps the Ligurian area supplied the original stocks. Despite its lack of potential for large open settlements, the Ligurian coast reflects contacts with surrounding areas throughout the Neolithic.

The only other carbon–14 dates for Square-Mouthed Pottery in Liguria come from Level IX at Arma di Nasino, Val Pennevaira. Here a level containing both Square-Mouthed and *Cardium*-impressed sherds has five dates running from $4005 \pm 65$ b.c. (R316a) to $4520 \pm 120$ b.c. (R267) (Alessio, *et al,* 1968, pp. 354–6). The pottery is in association with wild fauna and marine molluscs. Sites in the same valley dating to the mid-fourth millennium b.c. (Arma dello Stefanin and Grotta del Pertusello) continue to produce remains of wild fauna (Leale Anfassi, 1958–61; 1962).

The square mouths and flat bases of the Ligurian Middle Neolithic are not found (with a few exceptions) in Provence and Languedoc; there is no question of cultural continuity between Liguria and Southern French areas at this period. However, a few decorative attributes are similar in the two areas: notched rims, geometric incised patterns of oblique 'ladders', or linear cross-hatched zones. The incised patterns are particularly important, since they are of frequent occurrence in both cultures and practically identical in design attribute. Roudil (1973) has suggested that incised decoration derived from the impressed in some cases (for instance the standard zig-zag from the pivoting impressed design), and provided an alternative to painting the same geometric designs in South Italy (the incised lines were the key to hold white or red filler against the dark background). This would account for the similarity of design elements in the two adjacent areas despite an overall variation in

*(Above)* Megalithic tomb of
Tiergus, St Affrique (Aveyron)
*(Photograph by Costantini)*

*(Opposite)* Middle gorges of
Verdon river: Grotte Murée
appears at the left of the second
photograph

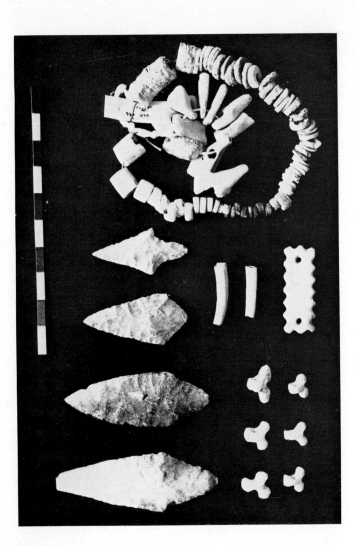

Arrowheads, winged beads and pendants of the Chalcolithic of the Grands Causses. Scale in cm. (*Photograph by Costantini*)

assemblage; in both cases they would have been derived from the local Epi-Cardial.

For about five hundred years the Square-Mouthed Pottery culture persists on the Ligurian coast, while in Southern France the Chasséen culture develops and spreads. During the same period Cardial culture continues its development the far side of the Pyrenees, and so far as we know, in Corsica and Sardinia also. Majorca was occupied by 4000 b.c., but its cultural affinities are not known (Kopper and Waldren, 1967–8, p. 113). In Central and Southern Italy the Painted Pottery cultures continue their complex evolutionary path.

A number of French Epi-Cardial assemblages were discussed in the last chapter. At some of the sites mentioned, there is an assemblage stratified above the Epi-Cardial which heralds the Chasséen culture. At Font-Juvenal, Conques (Aude) the Epi-Cardial Level 12 is dated $3900 \pm 100$ b.c. (MC499) and the following Level 11, containing smooth-faced pottery of a 'pre-Languedocian Chasséen facies', $3590 \pm 100$ b.c. (MC498). At Camprafaud (Hérault) Level 15 produced S-walled, well-made vases bearing ring handles and cylindrical vases with flat lugs, accompanied by a flake industry on honey flint. This level probably dates to the early fourth millennium b.c. (Rodriguez, 1970, p. 20).

In the Aveyron the cave of Sargel I, St Rome de Cernon, produced an assemblage of finely made baggy pots with ring handles, and bowls, in Level XI of the 1965 excavation (Costantini, 1970, fig. 6), below a fully Chasséen assemblage. At the mouth of the Rhône, the level overlying the Epi-Cardial assemblage at Escanin 2, Les Baux, contains bowls and deep jars with flat lugs, and bladelets (Montjardin, 1966, figs. 22–9).

To the West of the Rhône a number of levels have been excavated with Epi-Cardial and Chasséen elements found in association, for example, rock-shelter 3 of St Mitre, Reillanne (Basses-Alpes), and the upper porch of the Grotte de l'Eglise, Baudinard (Var). The Eglise Supérieure cave in the Verdon valley Middle Gorges has produced one of the earliest dates for a Chasséen assemblage (Level 8B – $3810 \pm 140$ b.c. – Gif 1334). Level 8B lay on bedrock, so there is no fear of contamination from earlier levels. There are a number of *Cardium*-impressed sherds, but the majority of the pottery is Chasséen, and includes a multi-perforated cordon on a rim, carinated bowls, a conical strainer and an incised sherd. The finely retouched lozenge and leaf arrowheads include one made in

F

obsidian – the earliest dated instance of this material in Southern France. Flint transverse arrowheads, blades and a borer complete the lithic industry (Courtin, 1970, fig. 5).

Marked lithic and ceramic changes occur with the advent of the Chasséen culture. Probably this very complete and uniform assemblage alteration reflects systemic change in the culture and economy. It is postulated that the initial impact of domesticated products in the sixth and fifth millennia b.c. would be to reduce the resource areas of groups and allow for a steady population build-up without expansion. However, as the easier growing land was occupied or over-cropped, some groups might have felt the pressure to move inland and seek new pastures and farmland. This certainly seems to have happened in the early fourth millennium b.c., when new areas of Southern France (Verdon valley, Grands Causses) were colonized by farming groups.

In general, Chasséen pottery (Figures 8, 11) is a highly burnished, well finished ware, often in dark colours, although it can be red or even cream (pottery from La Madeleine cave, Monaco Museum). The main shapes are the low bowl, often with an incised horizontal line below the rim; the carinated bowl; the globular necked vase; and baggy jars. Rarer shapes include the brimmed plate and socketed cup ('vase-support'), both well decorated with incised designs before firing. The main designs are geometric – hatched or cross-hatched triangles or lozenges, 'ladders', or zig-zags. These patterns would be filled with white or red incrustation to stand out against the dark surface. Plastic decoration is also rich, in the form of neat pierced and non-pierced buttons, rather fewer handles, cordons with multiple perforations, and Pan-pipes (a series of clay tubes stuck on to the side of the vessel, usually the globular-necked vase). There are rare indented clay plaques, possibly anthropomorphic figurines (Figure 9).

This ceramic series is accompanied by a lithic industry with numerous small fine blades and bladelets, often in honey-coloured flint, of triangular or trapezoidal section. These comprise 50% of the industry at Grotte C in the Verdon valley (Courtin and Pélouard, 1971, p. 546) and 90 per cent at two sites on the plain near

*Figure 8. Chasséen pottery of the Gardon valley. Nos. 1, 4, 6–9, St Vérédème cave; No. 2, Baume Longue; No. 3, Baume Latrone; No. 5, St Joseph cave. Scale – half natural size.*

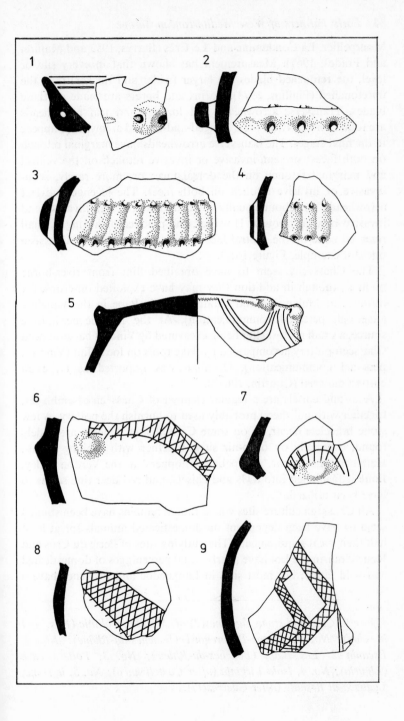

Montpellier, La Condamine and Le Crès (Barrès, 1953 and Majurel and Prades, 1967). Measurement has shown that in every site or level, the retouched blades are larger (wider and thicker) than the unretouched (Phillips, 1973). Burins and borers are made on these blades. Transverse arrowheads and lozenge and leaf arrowheads are found on nearly all sites. Tanged-and-barbed arrowheads appear in the final stages. The transverse arrowheads have marginal retouch on both faces; or semi-invasive or invasive retouch on the ventral and marginal retouch on the dorsal face; or, more rarely, semi-invasive or invasive retouch on both faces. The lozenge and leaf arrowheads are about equally divided between semi-invasive and invasive bifacial retouch. However, the practice of having a small reserved zone on the ventral face seems to be a typically Chasséen one (for example, Figure 16:2).

The Chasséens seem to have obtained flint from river-borne nodules, though in addition they may have exploited outcrops, for instance at Malaucène and Châteauneuf-du-Pape in the Vaucluse (Aspinall, personal communication). At the Malaucène hillside source, a small rock-shelter being excavated by Vincent has produced Chasséen pottery accompanied by flake tools on local flint (Vincent, personal communication). Obsidian was imported as an extra cutting material (Courtin, 1967b).

Axes and chisels are a regular element of Chasséen assemblages, together with polishers, probably used to burnish the pottery. A few stone bracelets occur, as on some Cardial sites. Querns are widely found, especially on open-air sites, together with rubbing stones. Hammerstones occur, and pebble 'choppers' in the Verdon valley. Bone is fashioned into awls and chisels, and red deer tine seems to have been utilized.

All Chasséen culture sites whose faunal remains have been studied seem to have been dependent on domesticated animals for at least half their meat requirements. The outlying sites of Perte du Cros and Roucadour in the Lot have nearly equal percentages of domesticated and wild fauna, but most sites in Languedoc and Provence have a

---

*Figure 9. Clay and stone figurines(?) of Middle Neolithic (Nos. 1–4 in clay). No. 1, Orgon-Beauregard (Bouches-du-Rhône); No. 2, Escanin 2, Les Baux (Bouches-du-Rhône); No. 3, Pollera cave (Liguria); No. 4, Isola Virginia (after Castelfranco); No. 5, in stone, Lagozza di Besnate (after Guerreschi).*

definite preponderance of domesticated beasts (Phillips, 1972, pp. 49–51). Animal domestication seems to have been on a sound footing in the Chasséen, with emphasis either on sheep-goat or cattle raising. Wild cattle are reported from the Lot department sites and from Grotte Sartanette in the Gardon valley, and red deer, boar and rabbit frequently appear in the faunal record.

Grain has been recovered in carbonized form from a number of sites (for example, Grotte de la Madeleine, Villeneuve-les-Maguelone – Hérault – and the Verdon valley sites). An impression on a sherd from the Chasséen levels of the Grotte de Gazel was identified as Emmer by Jane Renfrew (personal communication). The Chasséens seem to have grown Emmer and bread wheat and both types of barley, together with various beans and vetches (Courtin, 1974; Phillips, 1972, p. 52). Acorns were widely used, just as in Spain.

Where did the Chasséen culture first crystallize? Most likely to the West of the Rhône, where Guilaine has recently claimed that a 'proto-Chasséen' level exists at the Baume de Montbolo in the Pyrenees (Guilaine, 1970b; 1974). The globular pottery, sometimes decorated with vertically pierced long lugs, is found in association with querns and sheep bones (Guilaine, 1970b, pp. 156–7, pp. 166–9). Similar material was found some years ago in the same Pyrenaean area at the Montou cave, Corbières-les-Cabanes, but unfortunately remains unpublished. Even without Montbolo, the proto-Chasséen assemblages already mentioned are found to the West of the Rhône. Seven Chasséen sites West of the Rhône have carbon–14 dates from 3770 b.c. to 3140 b.c. (the caves of Camprafaud, Le Claux, La Madeleine and Bourbon, the porch site of La Perte du Cros, and the open-air settlements of St Michel-du-Touch and Roucadour). Only four Chasséen sites East of the Rhône have dates before 3000 b.c. (Grotte de l'Eglise Supérieure, Baume de Fontbrégoua, Abri 3 de St Mitre and the open-air site of Escanin 2). There are approximately twice as many Chasséen sites West of the Rhône (117) as East of it (63) (Phillips, 1971a). The largest sites, with putatively the greatest populations, are West of the Rhône (St Michel-du-Touch, Ville-neuve-Tolosane, La Condamine, Le Crès). This emphasis of occupation West of the Rhône probably means that the origin of the Chasséen lies there.

Only in Provence, to the East of the Rhône, does the Cardial culture seem to have lingered on until the turn of the fourth millennium b.c. Only in Provence are there sites with levels containing a majority of Chasséen sherds with an admixture of *Cardium*-impressed ones (Abri 3 de St Mitre, the upper and middle porches of Grotte de l'Eglise, and Grotte G, Baudinard – all in the Var department).

The Chasséen culture lasts from the early fourth to the mid-third millennium b.c. and is a remarkably homogenous one. Despite the fact that there are now a few series of dated Chasséen levels at Verdon valley sites, the La Madeleine cave, and the porch site of Perte du Cros, little assemblage variation can be traced over time. For one reason, most of the cave sites produce relatively small quantities of finds; for another, certain zones like the Verdon valley have proved to be regionally specialized in pottery within the overall unity of the Southern French Chasséen (Phillips, 1973). The Perte du Cros has produced the best-documented report of assemblage change (Galan, 1967), but lies on the outskirts of the Chasséen province.

The Verdon valley Middle Gorges figure largely in this discussion of the Chasséen culture, since the cliff walls of Kimmeridge-Portland limestone are honeycombed with caves and networks of galleries (Plate 2). Extensive excavations have been undertaken by Courtin, and a number of reports already published (Courtin, 1967a; Courtin and Pélouard, 1971). On the left bank, in the Var department, a steep descent half-way down the cliffside leads to the porches and galleries of the Grotte de l'Eglise; Grotte G lies fifty metres beyond. Grotte C opens just above river level at the foot of the gorges (Figure 10). On the right bank, almost opposite Grotte C, lies the Grotte Murée. Further upstream, on the same side as the Grotte Murée and therefore in the Basses-Alpes department, the Abri du Jardin du Capitaine lies at the river's edge.

The various caves have approximately the following floor space: Grotte G, 10 m$^2$; Grotte de l'Eglise, upper porch, 30 m$^2$; Grotte C and Grotte Murée, 50 m$^2$; Grotte de l'Eglise, middle porch, 60 m$^2$; Abri du Jardin du Capitaine several 100 m$^2$. It has been estimated that they may have housed six to fifteen inhabitants (Phillips, 1972). Galleries leading from the upper porch of the Grotte de l'Eglise have been painted with rayed sinuous designs (Courtin, 1961b), and these may date to the Chasséen occupation. The inhabitants seem to have grown a variety of wheats, barley and legumes and bred cattle and sheep-goat; they also collected acorns and hunted a small number of red deer, boar, ibex and rabbit (Courtin, 1974). Although many of these activities must presumably have taken place on the plateau above the gorges, no sign of Neolithic presence has ever been located there (Courtin, personal communication).

It has been possible to distinguish regional specialities in the Verdon valley ceramic types ('attribute clusters') (Phillips, 1972, p. 547). These include shouldered bowls with a small button on the shoulder, carinated bowls, some with a tunnel lug on the carination, and multi-perforated lugs on jar rims. In another valley area, that of the Gardon, the elaborate Cardial decoration described in the last chapter gave way to a rich variety of Chasséen, with emphasis on incised decoration of cross-hatched triangles and linear zones on the outside of bowls, and on Pan-pipes sometimes linkèd by flat cordons – on the walls of necked globular vessels (Figure 8).

Another area colonized by farmers for the first time in the Chasséen is the Grands Causses region. The Causses or plateaux of Larzac and Méjean and the Causse Noir are separated by deep valleys through which run a number of rivers, and the limestone walls of the cliffs encircling them contain many caves. As in the Verdon valley area, the Chasséens seem to have occupied mainly the cliff caves (Maury, 1967a). However, Costantini, who has excavated the Sargel I cave overlooking the Cernon river, claims there are two open-air Chasséen sites on the Causse de Larzac. There are probably over forty Chasséen sites in the Causses area (Maury, 1967a; Lorblanchet, 1965). Although much of the material is from non-stratified excavations it has been possible to see regional specializations in the pottery – firstly high numbers of multi-perforated cordons, and secondly, low bowls with elaborate internal decoration of hatched and cross-hatched zones, triangles and bands. Similar bowls are found in the adjoining Lot department at La Perte du Cros and Grotte du Noyer (for example, Clottes and Lorblanchet, 1972, p. 150).

Chasséen occupation also spread rapidly up to the Rhône valley, where it produced linked cultures in the Paris Basin, Jura-Burgundy and Swiss regions.

Both caves and open-air locations were chosen for occupation. A number of sites seem to have been located on the edge of former marshes or lagoons (for example, Salernes, Var department; Trets, Bouches-du-Rhône department; Le Grès-d'Orange, Vaucluse department). In the latter area irregular cobbled areas have been discovered recently, associated with a mass of small mollusc shells and Chasséen pottery and flints (Figure 11). One of these cobbled areas is situated above a pit dug down to the most recent Rhône

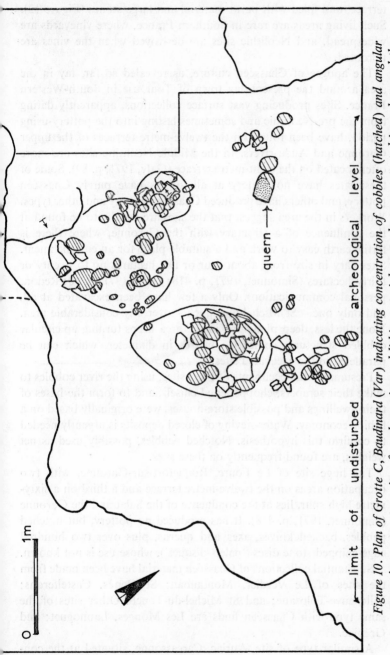

quern →

← limit of undisturbed        archeological level

Figure 10. Plan of Grotte C, Baudinard (Var) indicating concentration of cobbles (hatched) and angular
stones in or near two pits; faunal remains and lithic material were also concentrated in and around the
pits, while pottery was more generally distributed over the cave area (after Courtin and Pélouard).

terrace, and filled with burnt material and large stones (Figure 12). Such living areas are rare in Southern France, where vineyards are widespread, and Neolithic sites are destroyed when the vines are uprooted.

The apogee of Chasséen culture, as revealed so far, lay in the area around the present-day town of Toulouse in South-Western France. Sites producing vast surface collections, apparently dating from the pre-Neolithic and sometimes lasting into the pottery-using period, have been found on the twelve-metre terraces of the upper Garonne and Aude rivers. In the Middle Neolithic sites are more often located on the eight-metre terrace (Galy, 1971, p. 89). Some of these sites have no pottery at all, others have purely Chasséen pottery, and others have produced Chasséen pottery and other types. Workers in the area suggest that the sites are usually to be found at the confluence of a tributary with the Garonne, where there is fertile earth easy to work and a suitable place for an entrenchment. Sites vary in size from about four or five hectares up to twenty or thirty hectares (Simonnet, 1971, p. 418; Galy, 1971, p. 90; Redon, personal communication). Only a few have been excavated at all, and only one – St Michel-du-Touch – over any considerable area. None the less, deep ploughing in the area keeps turning up circular cobbled structures some two metres in diameter, which can be paralleled in the excavated sites.

Presumably the occupants of these sites, using the river cobbles to make their scrapers, choppers and chisels, and to form the bases of their dwellings and possible store-houses, were originally based on a fishing economy. Water-sieving of closed deposits is urgently needed to confirm this hypothesis. Notched pebbles, possibly used as net weights, are found frequently on these sites.

The huge site of Le Fourc, Roquefort-sur-Garonne, with two occupation areas on the twelve-metre terrace and a third on a sixty-metre high spur, lies at the confluence of the Salat and the Garonne (Simonnet, 1971, p. 418). It has produced no pottery, but notched pebbles, backed knives, axes and querns, plus over two hundred edge-chipped stone discs ('palets-disques'), whose use is not known.

Substantial collections of Chasséen material have been made from the sites of Le Verdier, Montauban; St Genès, Castelferons; Villeneuve-Tolosane; and St Michel-du-Touch. Other sites of the same type with Chasséen finds are Les Monges, Launoguet; and Grépiac.

A similar type of site, Auriac, Carcassonne, situated at the con-

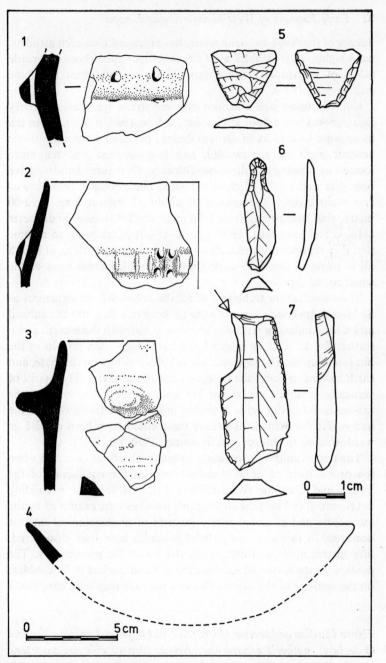

*Figure 11. Pottery and flint-work from Le Grès d'Orange (Vaucluse), author's excavations.*

fluence of the Aude and Jean rivers, has produced Chasséen artifacts, net weights, river cobbles used to make floors, and bones of cattle (45% of individuals) and sheep (36%), pig and goat (Guilaine and Vaquer, 1973).

Cobbled floors are a feature of these river-edge sites. A quarry face exposed half a floor at Grépiac (Méroc, 1959, p. 137), about ten more were located at St Genès (Redon, personal communication); another eight were excavated, and two hundred and ten more located by probing at Villeneuve-Tolosane. Over three hundred have been discovered at St Michel-du-Touch. These cobbled floors are of two main types, sub-rectangular, about 12 metres long by 2·50 metre wide, and round, from 0·80 metres to 1·80 metres in diameter (Méroc and Simonnet, 1970, pp. 38–41). It is tempting to assume that they represent respectively dwelling and storage places, although all but one of the Villeneuve-Tolosane cobbled areas were of the small round type.

The construction technique of all the cobbled-floor structures at St Michel-du-Touch was the same; a hole was dug into the subsoil and a fire kindled in it; the ashes were mixed with fresh earth and a further fire kindled, of which large burnt logs often remain in the hut foundations. The layer of river cobbles was laid on this base, and earth heaped to about the topmost limit of the cavity. The marks of vertically arranged sticks and branches preserved in some of the fire-hardened cavity walls probably indicates the framework of the hut walls; the excavators believe these could have been of pisé or wattle-and-daub (Méroc and Simonnet, 1970, pp. 41–3).

The opportunity of excavating so many structures occurred when the promontory of St Michel-du-Touch, at the confluence of the Touch and Garonne rivers (Figure 13), was sold for a building development in 1964; the contractor's trenches were examined by the excavators and extended where features of archaeological interest occurred. In this way two parallel palisades have been discovered, fifty metres apart and cutting off the tip of the promontory. The posts were stuck two metres into the soil and packed in by cobbles; on the analogy of the Mount Pleasant palisade they may have stood

---

*Figure 12. Plan and section of irregular 'hut floor' at Le Grès d'Orange (Vaucluse), author's excavations. No. 1, plan of cobbles, sandstone (hatched) and artifacts (solid black, p = pottery, f = flint); No. 2, section showing pit below floor.*

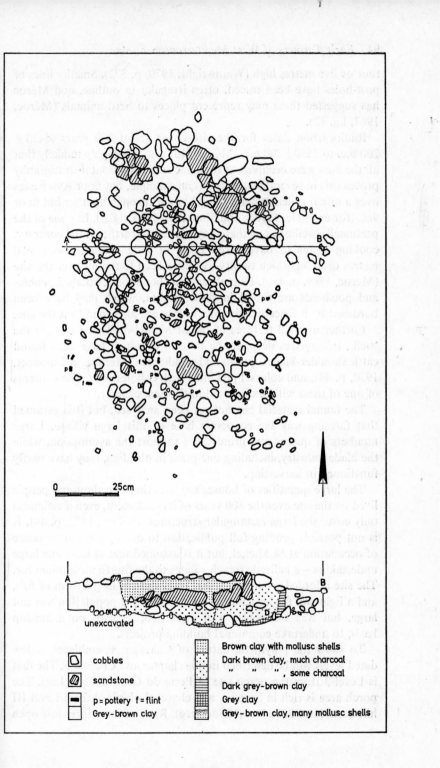

```
                    0        25cm
```

A ───────────────── B

unexcavated

| | Brown clay with mollusc shells |
| --- | --- |
| ▢ cobbles | Dark brown clay, much charcoal |
| ▨ sandstone | " " " , some charcoal |
| ▬ p = pottery  f = flint | Dark grey-brown clay |
| Grey-brown clay | Grey clay |
| | Grey-brown clay, many mollusc shells |

four or five metres high (Wainwright, 1970, p. 322). Smaller lines of post-holes have been traced, often irregular in outline, and Méroc has suggested these may represent places to herd animals (Méroc, 1967, fig. 12).

Radiocarbon dates for the site cover about 800 years (3430 ± 200 b.c. to 2550 ± 200 b.c., MC109, 102), so it is highly unlikely that all the huts were occupied at the same time. Horizontal stratigraphy proves this in several instances: as an example, hut floor A96 passes over a ditch, which a metre away has cut through another hut floor 96C (for example, Méroc and Simonnet, 1970, fig. 8). In none of the presumed dwellings was there any sign of a hearth; on the contrary, cooking seems to have taken place in wide ditches, about 0·80 metres deep, of which twenty-five have been found all over the site (Méroc, 1969, p. 486). Faunal remains, bone tools, notched pebbles and potsherds are found in these ditches, which may have been bordered by a fence or windbreak. Pits are also found on the site.

Further unusual features of the St Michel-du-Touch site are the 'well', 1·50 metres deep, at the bottom of which have been found cattle shoulder-blades, querns and grindstones (Méroc and Simonnet, 1970, p. 44), and colossal pits filled with cobblestones. The contents of one of these will be discussed in the next chapter.

The faunal material has not yet been analysed, but it is assumed that farming was the economic base of this large village. Large numbers of querns and grindstones support the assumption, while the blade industry, including one piece in obsidian, may have partly functioned in harvesting.

The large quantities of houses suggests that two thousand people lived on the site over the 800 years of its settlement, even if estimates only cover the large rectangular structures (Phillips, 1972, p. 44). It is not possible pending full publication to distinguish the sequence of occupation at St Michel, but it is assumed that at least one large undertaking – a palisade trench – dates to the fourth millennium b.c. The site afforded security, natural food sources in the form of fish, and a light soil for agriculture. At this time the population was not large, but was sufficiently well organized, perhaps on a kinship basis, to undertake communal building projects.

To show the polythetic nature of Chasséen assemblages, a few dated levels will be described in this chapter and Chapter 5. The first is Level 3 from the porch site of Perte du Cros, Saillac (Lot). The porch area is rich in hearths, and charcoal obtained from Level III has been dated 3260 b.c. (Heidelberg). Rims of forty-three low open

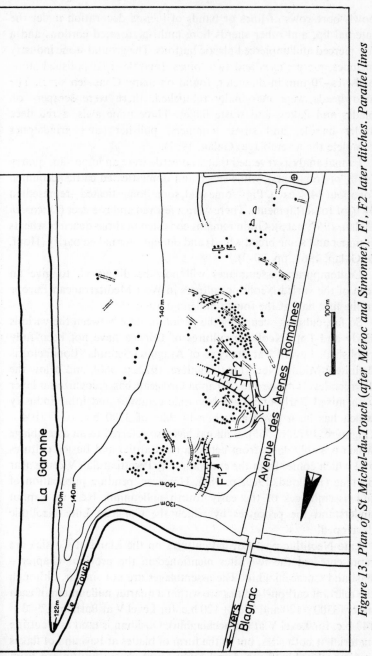

Figure 13. Plan of St Michel-du-Touch (after Méroc and Simonnet). F1, F2 later ditches. Parallel lines indicate sections of Chasséen ditches; where filled with dots, palisade trenches. Lunates indicate cobbled filled pits, one of them elaborate tomb. Black dots indicate hut floors.

bowls bore rows of lines or bands of incised decoration under the internal lip, and other sherds bore multi-perforated cordons and a few pierced and unpierced plastic buttons. The ground stone industry includes querns, axes and two 'billes' (marble-sized polished stone balls, 15–20 mm in diameter, found on many Chasséen sites). The arrowheads were marginally retouched, there were scrapers on blades and flakes, and waste flakes. Three bone awls, a red deer antler handle, and stone hammers, polishers and grindstones complete the assemblage (Galan, 1967).

Faunal analysis revealed that wild cattle were an important quarry (40% of fragments), while sheep and domesticated cattle accounted for about 14% each. Pig – some wild, some domesticated – represented 11% of total fragments. There were a few red and roe deer (Ducos, *in* Galan, 1967, p. 63). Grain remains consisted of three-quarters wheats (Emmer and some bread wheat) and one-quarter naked barley (Hopf, *in* Galan, 1967, pp. 70–3).

Contemporary assemblages will now be discussed, to give an idea of the varied Neolithic cultures in West Mediterranean Europe in the first half of the fourth millennium b.c.

So far, cultures occupying the period of time between the various Early and Late Neolithic cultures of Corsica have not been fully published. Level 15 at the cave of Araguina-Sennola (Bonifacio) is definitely Middle Neolithic (Gagnière, 1972, p. 566), and below the Torréen levels of the site of Tappa Grosjean has recognized a layer with mixed Early and Late Neolithic ceramics and lithic industry which has been given a carbon-14 date of 3700 b.c. (Gif 2104 – Gagnière, 1972, p. 565). Bailloud has also referred to an assemblage which possibly dates from between the Cardial and Basien cultures and which comes from the excavation by Peretti at San Vicente near Sartène (Bailloud, 1969, p. 384). However, pending publication of full assemblages of the early fourth millennium b.c., we cannot understand the processes by which the Corsican Late Neolithic developed.

Late Neolithic post-Cardial cultures on the island of Corsica are represented at the two sites mentioned in the previous chapter – Basi and Curacchiaghiu. The assemblages are not similar, although the relevant carbon-14 dates are within a quarter millennium of each other (3300 ± 120 and 3250 ± 120 b.c. for Level V at Basi, and 2980 ± 140 b.c. for Level V at Curacchiaghiu). Obsidian is used as a cutting material at both sites, but in the form of blades at Basi and of flakes at Curacchiaghiu. Tanged and barbed arrowheads are known from

Statue-menhirs
from Euzet-les-
Bains, Troujel
(Gard) and
Rosseironne,
Castelnau-Valence
(Gard) *(Photograph
courtesy of
Museum of Natural
History, Nîmes)*

*(Above)* The 'war dead' of
Roaix rock-cut tomb
(Vaucluse), upper level
*(Photograph by Courtin)*

*(Opposite)* Houses of
Fontbouïsse culture at
Cambous and La Conquette
(Hérault)

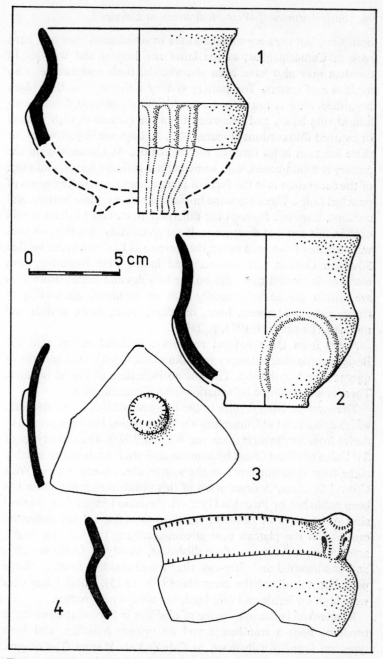

*Figure 14. Corsican and Sardinian Late Neolithic. Nos. 1, 2, Basi (after Bailloud); Nos. 3, 4, Sa Uca de Su Tintirriolu (after sketches by author in Sassari Museum).*

both sites, but they are manufactured in obsidian at Basi and hard rock at Curacchiaghiu; at the latter site lunates and trapezes in obsidian may also have been arrowheads. Both communities also made use of quartz. The pottery is very different – at Basi black burnished ware is found in carinated and shouldered forms, with hollow ring bases, and decorated from the carination with vertical or swathed thin cordons (Figures 14:1, 2). Lugs are bi-perforated, or there are twin holes through the carination. At Curacchiaghiu the pottery is round-based, with some necked globular forms, and most of the decoration is in the form of incised lines surrounding zones of punched holes. There are some bi-pierced buttons, plain buttons and cordons, however. Perhaps the difference in carbon-14 dates would explain this ceramic divergence. It seems unlikely that the two sites were isolated from each other, the more so as Lanfranchi claims that Southern Corsica was well-occupied in the Late Neolithic, with many open-air and cave sites on the hillsides and buttes. Both sites are within the same naturally rich environment, abounding in fruits, nuts, wild sheep, boar, red deer, trout, birds, seafish and molluscs (Lanfranchi, 1973, p. 213).

Apart from these natural resources, Bailloud claims that the Basien people were sedentary agriculturalists, based on the quantity of querns found at the site. There is no indication of faunal remains. There is no economic information from Curacchiaghiu.

The most unifying feature in the two assemblages is the obsidian, which at Basi and at Curacchiaghiu at this period has been proved to derive from Sardinia (Hallam and Warren, 1973). The three types of Sardinian obsidian found by neutron activation analysis presumably come from different flows at the source site, Monte Arci in West Central Sardinia. A description of this obsidian-rich mountain has been published by Puxeddu (1955–7). Puxeddu located four original sites or quarries of obsidian on the mountainside, ten collecting centres (on the plateau near streams carrying the volcanic rock), seventy-two workshops of smallish size, mostly in fertile country, and one-hundred and sixty-two sites where obsidian formed a large part, but not all, of the assemblage (Figure 15). These latter sites were both on fertile and arid land, but always near routes.

Monte Arci is the sole source of obsidian in Sardinia; however, it produces both a translucent and an opaque obsidian, and both types are found, for instance, at Cala di Vela Marina. The origins, development and close of the Sardinian obsidian trade are of considerable interest. Contributions to this study have already been

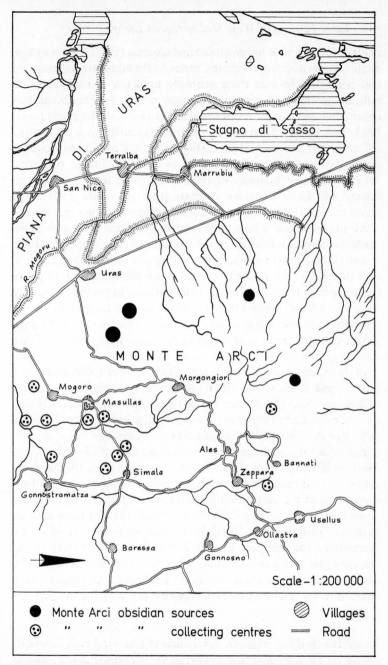

*Figure 15. Monte Arci. Central Western Sardinia. Plan of obsidian sources (solid black) and collecting centres (dot-filled circles). After Puxeddu.*

made by Cann and Renfrew (1964) and Courtin (1967b). The present picture shows obsidian reaching Corsica by the mid-sixth millennium, and being widely used there probably until the end of the third millennium (Hallam, personal communication). In France, on the other hand, the earliest dated obsidian artifact is the lozenge arrowhead from Level 8B, Grotte de l'Eglise, Baudinard (Var) (Courtin, 1970, fig. 5.6) dated to 3810 b.c. (Figure 16:2). Courtin has reported on the 114 obsidian artifacts known in Southern France (Courtin, 1967b). The vast majority of these finds come from East of the Rhône and from Chasséen contexts (that is, before 2500 b.c.); however, in 1973 Sauzade and Courtin discovered two leaf arrowheads in obsidian in a megalithic tomb in Provence, and an obsidian blade is reported from a post-Chasséen level at the Grotte de Labeil (Hérault). These later finds still remain to be analysed, but if they prove, like the majority of French obsidian artifacts, to come from Sardinia (Hallam, Warren and Renfrew, in preparation), this suggests that the obsidian 'trade' trickled on into the second half of the third millennium b.c. In this connection it is interesting to note that a nucleus found near Valencia was also from a Chalcolithic context (Jorda, 1959, fig. 123).

In Northern Italy Renfrew and Cann analysed obsidian from Isolino and Pescale; the latter site probably dates to the fourth millennium b.c. The former has a long stratigraphy but Barfield dates the obsidian artifacts to the Square-Mouthed horizon (Barfield, 1971, p. 46). The obsidian is Sardinian.

The relatively small numbers of obsidian artifacts found outside Sardinia have travelled a considerable distance from their source. Since Central and Southern Italy seem to have drawn their supplies from the closer Pontine Islands and Lipari (for example, Arias-Radi, *et al*, 1972, p. 165) it seems likely that the trade path of Sardinian obsidian was North to Corsica and via that island to North Italy and Southern France. The individualistic nature of the pottery types in all these regions while the trade was at its height (mid-fourth to mid-third millennia b.c.) suggests that contacts were not influential at a cultural level. Obsidian was a useful and perhaps

---

*Figure 16. Obsidian artifacts. No. 1, Basi (Corsica); No. 2, Level 8B, Grotte de l'Eglise, Baudinard (Var) (after Courtin); No. 3, Bovila Padro de Ripollet, cist grave 1 (after Ripoll and Llongueras); No. 4, Le Grès d'Orange (Vaucluse).*

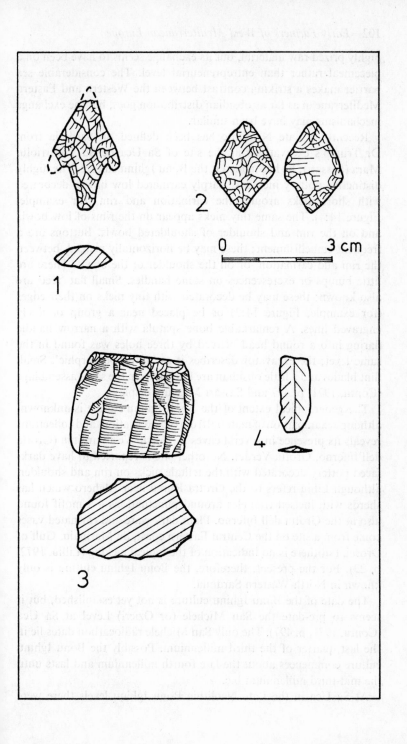

highly prized raw material, but its exchange seems to have been on a piecemeal rather than entrepreneurial level. The considerable sea barrier makes a striking contrast between the Western and Eastern Mediterranean as far as obsidian distribution goes, but the exchange mechanisms may have been similar.

Recently a Late Neolithic has been defined on Sardinia from Dr Trump's excavations at the site of Sa Uca de Su Tintirriolu, Mara (Sassari); he has named it the Bonu Ighinu culture. The highly distinctive pottery includes sharply carinated low bowls, decorated with short nicks around the carination and rim (for example, Figure 14:4). The same tiny nicks appear on the rims of low bowls and on the rim and shoulder of shouldered bowls. Buttons are a frequent embellishment; these may be horizontally pierced, between the rim and carination, or on the shoulder of the bowls. There are little bumps or excrescences on some handles. Small flat 'feet' are also known; these may be decorated with tiny nicks on their edges (for example, Figure 14:3) or be placed near a group of finely engraved lines. A remarkable bone spatula with a narrow handle flaring into a round head pierced by three holes was found in the same level; the excavator describes it as 'anthropomorphic'. Small flint blades and a little obsidian are known from the same assemblage (Contu, 1971, p. 497 and Sassari Museum display).

The geographical extent of the Bonu Ighinu culture is unknown, although examination of material from old excavations and collections reveals its presence in several caves in North-West Sardinia (Grotta dell'Inferno, Grotta Verde). No other site is reported to have dark-faced pottery decorated with the telltale nicks on rim and shoulder, although Lilliu refers to the Grotta Rureu near Alghero which has sherds with incised triangles around punctuations – a motif found also at the Grotta dell'Inferno. Plain dark ware and carinated vases come from a site on the Central Eastern coast, Su Marinaiu, Gulf of Orosei, but there is no indication of the typical nicking (Lilliu, 1972, p. 23). For the present, therefore, the Bonu Ighinu culture is only known in North-Western Sardinia.

The date of the Bonu Ighinu culture is not yet established, but it seems to pre-date the San Michele (or Ozieri) Level at Sa Uca (Contu, 1971, p. 497). The only San Michele radiocarbon dates lie in the last quarter of the third millennium. Possibly the Bonu Ighinu culture commences about the late fourth millennium and lasts until the mid-third millennium b.c.

At Sa Uca in the Late Neolithic Bonu Ighinu levels there were large quantities of shells and few bones (Don Renato Loria, personal communication). The Su Marinaiu site (Lilliu, 1972, p. 23) produced the dark undecorated pottery mentioned above in association with obsidian flakes and blades, a few fish and animal remains (goat, boar), and many marine molluscs, especially *Patella ferruginea*.

With the clear definition of a Sardinian Late Neolithic at the Sa Uca cave, the time has come to cease describing Sardinian dark-faced pottery as being of 'Chassey' or 'Bougon' or 'Fontbouïsse' type (for example, Lilliu, 1972, p. 24). Since they were first mooted (Audibert, 1958), the terms themselves have been much more pre-cisely formulated in France, and seen to belong to cultures widely dispersed in space and time. The links seen by Audibert were of single attributes (perforated buttons and so on). No assemblage found in Sardinia has the same grouping of form and decorative attributes as the Chasséen of Southern France, much less the Languedocian Fontbouïsse culture. Sardinian archaeologists do not claim that there was direct cultural influence between Southern France and Sardinia, but that these individual elements represent partial imports following trade. The above discussion on the obsidian trade, while admittedly tentative, concluded that direct Franco-Sardinian links were unproven and not inherently likely. The form of the typological similarities (their individual nature) and the possibility of finding similar single-attribute similarities in other neighbouring cultures in Corsica or Southern Italy add strength to this conclusion.

Throughout the fourth millennium b.c. ditched settlements and caves continued to be occupied in Southern Italy. In Central Italy part of the open-air site excavated by the Pisa school at Ripoli, Vibrata valley (Abruzzo) has been dated to the last quarter of the fourth millennium b.c. Ripoli is a famous open-air site where pits (supposedly dwellings) have been excavated since the middle of the nineteenth century (Cremonesi, 1965). In recent years, a flat-bottomed ditch, re-cut three times, was discovered, running around that part of the site which has been investigated. The various phases of development are not known from excavation but the material from three groups of pits was sufficiently different to warrant sep-arating them on chronological grounds. This separation has been more or less upheld by radiocarbon dates, which have dated Pit 12 of Group 1 to $3680 \pm 80$ b.c. (R–664), Pit 6 of Group 2 to $3610 \pm 150$ b.c. (R–665) and Pit 3 of Group 3 to $3150 \pm 120$ b.c. (Azzi, *et al*, 1973). Group 3 pits, more or less contemporary with the French and

Corsican sites already described, contained an industry based on obsidian and pottery described as having relationships with that of the Lagozza and Diana cultures, which will be briefly described below. Pit 3 contained only potsherds bearing tubular lugs, or lugs with raised edges, tronconic vessels with a cylindrical collar, some nail and dot-impression and a few incised sherds. Bones from Pit 3 were analysed to give the following numbers of fragments: 57 sheep-goat, 40 pig and 30 cattle, plus 9 red deer and 7 roe deer. In general there was a slight drop in pig percentages and a slight rise in wild animal remains in Group 3 over Group 1 (Cremonesi, 1965, pp. 153–4).

The Diana culture was defined by Professor Bernabò Brea during excavations in the early 1950s on the acropolis and Contrada Diana plain sites of the island of Lipari, near Sicily (Bernabò Brea and Cavalier, 1960). The acropolis had been mainly occupied earlier in the fourth millennium b.c., first by people using trichrome pottery and secondly by people using Serra d'Alto ceramics (fine *figulina* ware decorated with spiral-meander or lozenge, triangle or zigzag painted motifs and with elaborate scroll handles). The trichrome pottery has already been mentioned, and the Serra d'Alto wares are also widely spread on Sicily and the mainland from about 3500 to 2500 b.c. (Whitehouse, 1969, pp. 287–93). There was a limited occupation of the acropolis during the Late Neolithic, dated to $3050 \pm$ 200 b.c. (R180), but a much more intensive occupation was named after the Contrada Diana site, on the plain between the acropolis and the hills (Bernabò Brea and Cavalier, 1960, fig. 1). Here, at a level dated $2935 \pm 55$ b.c. (R182), monochrome red pottery was produced in a series of wide low bowls with rolled-out rims, deeper jars, and trono-conic bowls. Trumpet lugs with flared ends or lugs with raised edges decorate the pottery. The rest of the assemblage consisted of a blade industry on obsidian, which is found on Lipari; ground stone axes, chisels and pounders; querns and grind-stones; loom-weights and spindle-whorls; and fragments of copper slag.

Just as the Diana ware, in its distinctive red slip, recurs in assemblages of the end of the fourth millennium b.c. in Southern and Central Italy, so does dark-faced Lagozza ware in the North and on some Central Italian sites. Its ramification and artifact links will be discussed in the next chapter.

At the end of the fourth millennium b.c. a number of technological and perhaps religious events were taking place in Southern Italy: copper slag, as found at Lipari, was a by-product of the earliest metal-working, which will be described more fully in the next chapter; rock-cut tombs were a new form of construction to house the dead. Whitehouse suggests that the earliest instance of this fashion is to be found on the Foggia plain at Fonteviva, opening out of the side of the inner of two concentric ditches (Whitehouse, 1972, p. 276). Three damaged tombs were found at Pizzone in Taranto; at both sites Impressed Ware was found, with Burnished Ware at Fonteviva and with Matera Scratched Ware and a little *figulina* at Pizzone. There seems little doubt that these tombs were constructed in the fourth millennium b.c.

Radiocarbon dates for the Zebbug phase, in which the earliest Maltese rock-cut tombs occur, also fall into the fourth millennium b.c. ($3190 \pm 150$ and $3050 \pm 150$ b.c. – BM 145, 147 – Whitehouse, 1972, p. 278).

Similar early dates probably apply to the first rock-cut tombs in Portugal; this contemporaneity of Italian and Portuguese dates, and the evolution that can be seen between the rock-cut and the megalithic form in the Alentejo and in South-East Spain, suggest a local evolution in Iberia.

The Cardial culture seems to have developed slowly throughout much of the fourth millennium b.c. on the Eastern Spanish seaboard, and some of the ceramic styles described in the last chapter may date to this millennium. Due to lack of stratigraphy, it is not certain if the dark-faced pottery found in caves near the monastery of Montserrat was contemporary with the *Cardium* decorated ware, or posterior to it. Because of the Montbolo stratigraphy, it is probably possible to assign vertically pierced, smoothly burnished handles on carinated vases from the Cova Freda to the fourth millennium (Figure 17:8). A multi-perforated cordon from Cova Gran provides a link with the Chasséen, as do honey-coloured blades, transverse arrowheads and potsherds with pierced buttons from Level A at Toll de Moya (Muñoz, 1965, pp. 220–2); however, we cannot date these finds more closely than *circa* 3500 to *circa* 2500 b.c. (Figures 17:2, 3, 6, 7, 9, 10).

In the Valencia area, the regional quality of the pottery probably remained remarkably undisturbed, because some of its features, such as 'twinned' vases, recur in Bronze Age contexts (villages of La Atalyuela, Losa del Obispo, Ereta de Castellar and Mola Alta de Serelles, Alcoy – Valencia Prehistory Museum and, for example, Arnal, Prades and Fletcher, 1968, fig. XIV.4). The exceptional richness and complexity of decoration of the *Cardium*-impressed pots may reflect this longevity and security. Connections with the

South are indicated by a red-slipped vessel with vertically pierced lug incised with cross-hatching and swathes of incision found at La Sarsa (San Valero, 1950, plate X.2). However, as the Los Murciélagos stratigraphy has shown, this could date from any time after 4300 b.c.

Twenty-five kilometres from the La Sarsa cave, surface collections on the low sandhill of Casa de Lara produced *Cardium*-impressed pottery and laterally pierced *Nassa* and *Columbella* shells, as well as incised pottery, strainers and plaque flint. It is assumed that the makers of Cardial pottery occupied the hill when it was close to a marsh, and that subsequent occupants (presumably in the fourth or third millennia b.c.) continued to find it an advantageous setting (Soler Garcia [not dated]).

In the South of Spain relative chronology during the Neolithic is relatively well known, due to stratigraphic excavations in the caves of Nerja, Cariguela del Piñar and Los Murciélagos. In Chamber 1 of the Nerja cave a pit 40 cm deep and a metre in diameter, perhaps originally lined with irregular limestone slabs, contained thirty litres of cereals and acorns. Just over 85% by weight were naked barley, and most of the remaining quantity wheat, probably Emmer (Hopf and Pellicer, 1970). Olives and acorns were also represented. A red-painted sherd was found on the floor of this pit, which has been dated by radiocarbon assay of the cereals to $3115 \pm 40$ (Groningen). The pit was dug into Level 1C from Level 1B (Pellicer, 1963, p. 18). Level 1B contained bellied vases in fine ware, with a conical base and large and small blades. Red painted and incised pottery and stone bracelets were already present in the earlier Levels II and IC. Similar stratigraphies in Chambers 2 and 5 at Nerja seem to confirm the persistence of mostly incised (and a little impressed) and red-slipped ware. Bracelets in limestone and *Pectunculus* shell continue to be important in IB.

Large quantities of limpet and pecten were obtained from the Nerja cave, plus small animal bones (so far unidentified). An analysis of the fauna by level should clarify the degree to which the inhabi-

*Figure 17. Middle to Late Neolithic of the Barcelona region. Nos. 1–7, shell bracelet, transverse arrowheads, bone spoon and potsherds from Toll de Moya, Moya; Nos. 8, 9, vertically and horizontally pierced lugs from Cova Freda, Montserrat; No. 10, multi-perforated lug from Cova Gran, Montserrat. Scale – half natural size.*

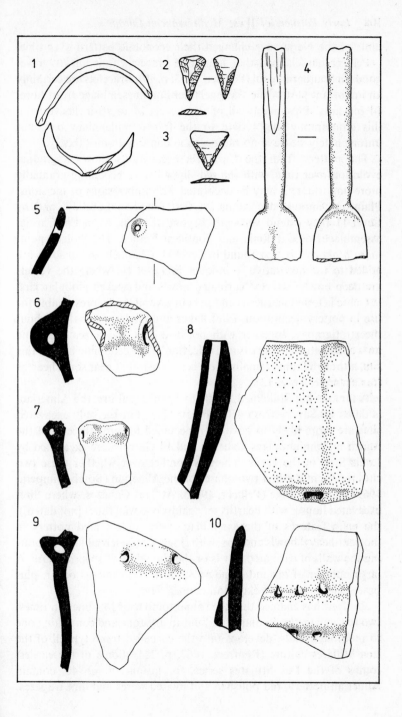

tants of the Nerja cave changed their economic pattern over time.

Pellicer has claimed that limestone bracelets function as grave-goods in Southern Spain (Pellicer, 1963, p. 40). Bracelets are certainly an important part of the Cariguela del Piñar assemblage from Level 14 onwards. Presumably all of the Levels 14 to 10 inclusive from this stratigraphy might date to the fourth millennium b.c., but unfortunately we have no radiocarbon confirmation of this.

The pottery from the Cariguela excavations shows a gradual evolution over time, with the red-slipped ware becoming gradually more important; it may be decorated with impressions or incisions. Plain and impressed cordons are first found in Level 13, and by Level 11 they extend vertically beyond the rim, as in Epi-Cardial assemblages of Catalonia and Southern France. The 'holed spout' (*ansa a pitorro*) is first found in Level 11. Channels and grooves are added to the decorative techniques in Level 10, where the vessels are deep bowls, inverted carinated bowls and necked globular jars.

Ochre is found in querns and pots in several levels, presumably for use in pottery decoration. Flint flakes and blades occur throughout the stratigraphy, together with polished axes and adzes and bone awls and spatulae. There is no indication of the economic base at this site, although faunal remains were certainly found near some hearths (for example, Level 12).

A famous but ill-defined Southern Spanish culture, the Almerian, is dated by Savory from 4500 to 3500 b.c., but the only excavated sites are more likely to have been occupied towards the end of the fourth millennium. Tres Cabezos and El Garcel were excavated by Louis Siret in the 1880s. There is conflict over whether these two sites represent the first two phases of the Almerian (Bosch-Gimpera, 1969) or a late stage (Pellicer, 1967). At Tres Cabezos, where Siret excavated houses with hearths set against one wall (Siret [not dated]), the main features of the assemblage were undecorated pottery in 'bottom-heavy' bowls and jars, with singly or bi-pierced lugs decorating the walls of carinated bowls or the shoulders of spherical jars. A large number of ground stone axes, chisels and querns occur, plus bracelets in stone and clay, and copper slag.

Renfrew has claimed that the round tomb used in Almerian times, two to three metres in diameter, built in drystone and containing one to multiple burials, develops into the corbelled tomb typical of the Los Millares culture (Renfrew, 1967, p. 284). Some of the earliest tombs of the Los Millares series, for instance tomb 40, contain Almerian pottery, red polished and incised wares and flint trapezes.

Thus the enigmatic Almerian may well have been one of the elements making up the thriving Los Millares culture of the third millennium b.c.

Guilaine and da Veiga have suggested that a typologically 'Middle Neolithic' series of assemblages can be detected in Portugal, including vessels decorated with hatched incised bands or punctuate impressions. The best known site is the cave of Furninha Peniche (Guilaine and da Veiga, 1970, p. 315). Buttons and lugs near and on the rim continue in fashion from the earlier local Neolithic. The megalithic site of Carapito I (carbon-14 date 2900 ± 40 – GrN 5110) has produced an Impressed Ware sherd, and possibly at some of the other early megalithic sites the old ceramic styles recur (Guilaine and da Veiga, 1970, p. 319), suggesting that the Cardial was in its final phase of development in the fourth millennium.

With regard to economy, the Nerja shell-fish have already been mentioned. Davidson has indicated the presence of great heaps of shells in the Bronze Age Levels at Cueva del Volcan del Faro (Davidson, 1972, p. 23). The undated site at Possanco, near Comporta, Portugal also produced great quantities of mussels and other shell-fish (*Tapes desussatus, Cardium edule* and so on). The living area apparently stretched over some 10 000 m² beside an earlier lagoon (Ribeiro and Sangmeister, 1967). The analogies of the pottery of this site are with the late Neolithic Alentejo grave finds, so that the gathering economy seems to remain important for a long time on the Iberian peninsula.

The beginnings of both rock-cut tombs and megalithic architecture in Iberia lie in the fourth millennium b.c. Radiocarbon dates and thermoluminescent dates have between them given relatively good backing to Vera Leisner's divisions of the Portuguese Neolithic (Leisner, 1967). Her Ia Cardial period now has a radiocarbon date of 4370 ± 350 b.c. (Sa 198) for the Salemas cave, with its trapezoidal microliths and pendants in mussel shell. In IIa, where ex-Mesolithic peoples begin building megaliths, the small chamber of Anta 2, Poco da Gateira Evora (Alentejo) produced backed points and trapezes dated to *circa* 3700–3800 b.c. (TL date 4510 ± 280 b.c.), (Leisner and Leisner, 1959, 205 and plate 38.5). A very similar thermoluminescent date (4440 ± 260 b.c. – *circa* 3600 b.c.) is given for another polygonal chamber at Gorginos 2, Evora (Alentejo) (Leisner and Leisner, 1959, p. 238 and plate 38.4); Whittle, 1973.

The large chambered tomb of Carapito I, Guarda (Beira Alta), assumed by Leisner to belong to this same early period, is dated by radiocarbon to $2900 \pm 40$ and $2640 \pm 65$ b.c. (Grn 5110, Groningen).

Leisner's IIb period covers the early passage graves in the Alentejo, with polygonal chambers and a low passage of two stones. Influences from the South-East at this time include red-slipped pottery and Almerian-type idols. Schist plaques with heads also make a first appearance. Recently a passage grave at Fragoas, Concelho Vila Nova de Paiva (Beira) has produced a carbon-14 date of $3110 \pm 50$ b.c. (Grn 4924) for the deepest part of the archaeological layer, overlying weathered granite rock (Vogel and Waterbolk, 1967, p. 133).

In period IIa lozenge arrowheads take over from transverse, and grave goods often include schist plaques with geometrical incised designs. Leisner wishes to date this phase to the second half of the third millennium b.c., but the rock-cut tomb of Carenque I, which – albeit in old excavations – produced a very typical assemblage for this phase, has been dated by thermoluminescence to the early fourth millennium ($3930 \pm 235$ b.c.), which would be around 3300 b.c. in radiocarbon years.

The rock-cut tombs of Portugal thus seem likely to have begun as early, or nearly as early, as the stone chambers, and to be part of a regional collective burial complex rather than an exotic schismic manifestation. In the Tagus valley, where they were very popular, a long passage led to the circular chamber. There was also an entrance into the top of the chamber which was covered by a slab (a partly megalithic construction). All shades of development between the completely rock-cut and completely megalithic tomb are described by the Leisners (1943, p. 289).

Savory believes that some of the earliest Iberian collective burial took place in the natural and rock-cut caves of Andalusia and Murcia (Savory, 1968, p. 90). The rock-cut tombs here are carved into the slope and approached by either a horizontal passage or a vertical shaft. No radiocarbon dates are available for them, but if the single Carenque I thermoluminescent date is accurate, they may also date to the last half of the fourth millennium b.c., as he believes.

The fourth millennium b.c. communities reveal a wide variety of economic practices, from continued emphasis on mollusc collection, for instance in Sardinia and Portugal, to mainly hunting and collecting, for instance in North Italy, or a fairly solid farming economy, as in Southern France. The best evidence for change comes from Southern France.

The contrast between the Cardial and the Chasséen cultures is an interesting one. The number of sites, and presumably of people, increases. Agriculture was already one of the components of Cardial culture economic strategy; the increase of axes in the Chasséen probably indicates greater felling activity for fields, and the increase of querns greater use of grain in the diet. The evidence for grain and domesticated animals correlates with the increase in querns, axes, denticulated blades and blades with sickle lustre to suggest a more agricultural base to the economy. The prevalence of bowls in the ceramic repertory may be accounted for if the basic food served was gruel (Matson, 1965, p. 208).

Chasséen people did not entirely discard hunting, and the piercing arrowhead is found from the earliest levels onwards in the Verdon valley sites. Possibly the local wild animal population was a threat in this frontier area, both to the domesticated beasts owned by the colonists and to their fields. It may also, or alternatively, suggest contests and warfare. However, no evidence survives to support the latter hypothesis, apart from the palisade fence at St Michel-du-Touch.

On the eve of the third millennium b.c. West Mediterranean Europe was organized into a number of largish cultural blocks, with a certain amount of isolation between them. Portugal was economically traditional, but architecturally precocious; farming probably flourished in a number of favoured areas of coastal Spain, especially the South-East. The Balearics were only just being drawn into the Spanish cultural sphere. North–South lines of trade passed from Sardinia to Corsica to Southern France and Northern Italy, but each of the four areas boasted individual material cultures and economic specialities. Southern and Central Italy, Sicily and Malta had perhaps stronger trade and cultural links. Although collective burial was making tentative headway in the two most widely separated areas, over most of West Mediterranean Europe the emphasis was still on single crouched burials. This must mean that the group was not yet more important than the individual, or the simple family. Elaborate kinship ties had not yet been forged; the power of the group, in life and death, was still not paramount.

# 5. The Third Millennium b.c.

Prolific, more ostentatious than their forbears, the Europeans of the third millennium b.c. bring to fruition the processes initiated in the preceding millennia. They more or less completely adopt a farming economy; they show a marked increase in numbers in certain favoured areas; and they provide their own memorials in massive collective burial chambers and gifts to the dead.

Third millennium b.c. populations gradually acquire more varied material culture in the form of jewellery or emblematic items, some of them in copper, gold or ivory. They create large-scale sculptures and elaborate stone architecture.

These processes work at different speeds in different areas, and it is only by the end of the millennium that they are generally complete. A crucial difference occurs from the rather isolated large cultures of the late fourth millennium b.c. By the late third millennium b.c. West Mediterranean Europe abounds with highly individualistic local cultures, subject to rapid change, which are none the less linked cross-culturally by very strong bonds based on similarity of burial practice and probably much more intensive trade and exchange.

Our knowledge of the fourth millennium b.c. in Iberia again concerns the houses of the dead (megalithic and rock-cut tombs and pit-graves) rather than those of the living. Limited stratigraphic excavations, linked with the rarity of carbon-14 dates, and very different developments in the various regions of the peninsula, make it impossible to generalize about cultural development.

In the Barcelona region, A. M. Muñoz has claimed that the pit-graves (*sepulcros de fosa*) date from *circa* 3500 to *circa* 2500 b.c. (Muñoz, 1965, p. 383). Pit-graves are either simple pits, pits under capstones or a variety of stones, or built cists, usually containing a single flexed burial. Up to fifty were found in a cemetery at the most extensive site, Bovila Madurell. Grave-goods include many callais beads, *Pectunculus* bracelets, querns, small chisels and axes (some in the local Gerona basalt), bone points, flint blades, and fragments of

'Temple' of Monte d'Accodi, Sassari (Sardinia), showing ramp and revetment walls

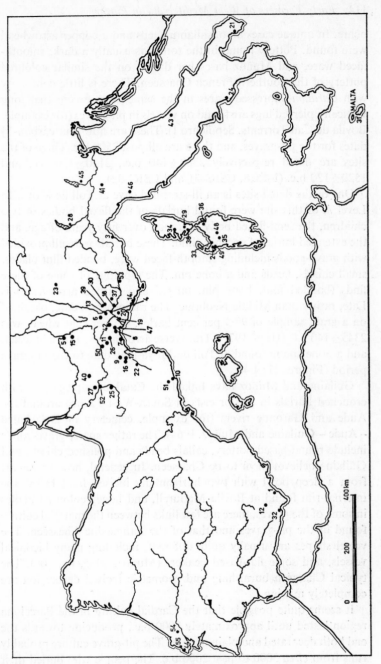

*Map 5 (see p. 15)*

ochre. In unique cases an obsidian nucleus and a copper arrowhead were found. Pottery found in the tombs is usually a dark, smooth-faced ware, and Muñoz bases her dating on the similar coloured pottery of the Southern French Chasséen. There is little continuity with *Cardium*-impressed wares in the same area, except that long vertically pierced lugs are found on vessels in pit graves (for example, Bovila de Can Torrents, Sepulchro I). There are now four carbon-14 dates for the pit-graves, and these are all post 2500 b.c. Three of the sites are dated respectively $2360 \pm 140$ b.c., $2120 \pm 130$ b.c. and $1520 \pm 120$ b.c. (I–1518, CSIC–31 and CSIC–32).

One of the dated sites is an ill-stratified cave at Toll de Moya. In Level A of this site were found burials of the flexed bodies of two children, the semi-flexed body of a man over fifty years of age, and the extended burial of another child. These burials were all provided with grave-goods including smooth-faced ware, banded flint blades, small chisels, beads and a bone pin. The typology of some of these finds (banded flint, bone pin, tanged and barbed arrowhead) is Late, rather than Middle Neolithic. The radiocarbon date, obtained on a grain sample of 99·5 per cent barley, 0·5 per cent wheat, was $2345 \pm 140$ b.c. (Hopf, 1971). Transverse arrowheads, a shell bracelet, and a bone spoon found at Toll de Moya may date to the pit-grave period (Figures 17: 1–4).

Guilaine and Muñoz have linked the Catalonian pit-graves with crouched burials in pits or cists in South-West France around the Aude and Garonne rivers (for example, cemetery of Dela-Laïga – Aude – Guilaine and Muñoz, 1964). The rather sparse grave-goods include round-based pottery, callais beads and polished chisels, and Guilaine believes them to be Chasséen. In general, however, apart from a deep bowl with two horizontally incised lines below the internal rim found at Bovila Madurell, and honey-coloured blades in some of the graves, there are few links between the material culture found in the pit-graves and that of the Languedoc Chasséen. The vessel shapes are usually quite different, including many biconical vessels, and some flat-based beakers (Muñoz, 1965, fig. 106). The typical Chasséen burnishing and geometric incised decoration are completely missing.

It seems quite possible that the Cardial culture in the Barcelona region lasted until approximately 3000 b.c., producing towards the end both decorated and plain pottery. The pit-grave culture probably runs from *circa* 3000 to past 2000 b.c. The people who buried their dead in pit-graves lived in open-air villages (there is an unconfirmed report of ten hut-floors having been found at Bovila Madurell). The cemeteries are all located in arable land (Ripoll and Llongueras, 1963, p. 70; Muñoz, 1965, p. 315). The presence of querns with the burials, plus bone awls made from sheep or goat, may be further indications of their farming status.

The quality of the grave-goods suggests a community of egalitarian type, with individuals being buried with their working tools. There are less sober elements in the tombs, especially the callais beads, and these may have been indications of some individual wealth or achieved status (Binford, 1962). If increased population encouraged the development of farming economy – which began as early as the mid-fifth millennium on the Eastern seaboard of Spain – this may have caused systematic change in the way of life of people who previously occupied caves high up in the hills behind the Barcelona plain. They probably opened up tracts of woodland with the basalt axes from the Gerona region which can be seen in their hundreds in the Sabadell Museum. Basalt may have been a valuable trade item, and in fact the wide variety of raw materials used to make axes suggests considerable trade (Maluquer de Motes, 1972, p. 33). Callais beads were deposited with the dead in sufficient numbers to suggest that this raw material was also easily obtained, and an important decorative or amuletic substance.

The people who used pit-graves to bury their dead were hardly influenced at all by the builders of megalithic tombs, whose burial type probably did not reach the Barcelona area until *circa* 2000 b.c.

Partly contemporary with the agriculturalists of the Catalonia pit-grave culture, a very homogenous cultural group extends from the Pyrenees to North Italy. In Southern France the Chasséen culture continues its development. At the foot of the middle gorges of the Verdon valley the Chasséen occupation of Grotte C, Baudinard has been dated to 2840 ± 140 b.c. (GsY 1621 – Courtin and Pélouard, 1971).

The main chamber of Grotte C is about 50 m², but a great deal of the fill was disturbed, and the finds only come from the rear 16 m², notably from two pits. Flint manufactures comprise three piercing and five transverse arrowheads, three borers and five burins (one of them opposed to one of the borers). A couple of river cobbles have been roughly broken to give a cutting edge. Three querns, an axe and stone ball ('bille') make up the ground stone industry, and six awls and two chisels are made of bone. The thousands of sherds include the rims of three hundred different vases, and thirty-seven

decorated sherds. Half the decoration consists of pierced and unpierced buttons, but there are also six multi-perforated cordons, a
Pan-pipe and a ring handle. Incised decoration appears around
plastic buttons and on bowl rims (Courtin and Pélouard 1971,
fig. 11).

Emmer, breadwheat and hulled barley grains were found in
carbonized form, and the faunal remains are divided between
56·09 % domesticated (23 individuals) and 43·91 % wild (18 individuals). This is an extremely high percentage of hunted species for the
Verdon valley caves, and, except for a single badger and a single
rabbit, these were all adult animals. By contrast half of the domesticated individuals, mostly sheep, followed by pig, were young or very
young (Poulain *in* Courtin and Pélouard, 1971, p. 563). Only three
cattle were represented, but these would have provided a considerable meat weight. The wide variety of animals hunted included
red deer, roe deer, boar, badger, wild-cat, and birds well known
until recently in Provence (wood-pigeon, grey partridge, magpie).
The domesticated animals are represented by many more fragments
than the wild, which suggests either that the relative economic
importance of the different species is being slightly distorted by the
figures of individuals represented, or that there was different butchering behaviour for the penned and hunted species.

A great contrast to the simple cave-dwellers of Grotte C is provided by the village of St Michel-du-Touch, already touched upon
in the last chapter. It seems likely that the greatest population and
most elaborate communal undertakings date to the later part of its
occupation. Among these features are huge pits filled with cobblestones. One of these was 32 m² in extent and 85 cm deep. At the
bottom, under the 25 m³ of cobblestones, were found the remains of
an adult and a child (Méroc, 1967, pp. 395–6). It is suggested that the
bodies were exposed before being put into the pit, since only parts
of the skeleton were found. The grave-goods, notably twelve complete pots, were found smashed under cobblestones, and it is suggested that a wooden structure originally covered skeletons and offer-
ings. The twelve pots represented two each of the following six
types – high-necked globular vases; brimmed plates; carinated
vases with Pan-pipes on the walls; flaring carinated bowls; open
bowls; and vase-supports (Méroc and Simonnet, 1970, p. 44). In
considerable contrast to this, on another part of the site, a woman
was found buried in a crouched position, accompanied by a tiny
vase containing four hedgehog jaws.

In the early third millennium b.c. there is greater continuity in artifact forms between Southern France and Liguria, as the Square-Mouthed pottery of the latter area is gradually replaced by Late Neolithic plain dark wares. At the Arene Candide cave Late Neolithic pottery appears in Levels 9 to 13 (Bernabò Brea, 1956, fig. 4). The date for levels 12–13 is $3125 \pm 45$ b.c. (R–104 – Alessio, *et al*, 1966, p. 402), but since underlying levels have two dates around 3050 b.c. there must be some doubt if the Late Neolithic occupation began before the early third millennium b.c. There is a similarity with the lithic of Chasséen assemblages, in that transverse arrowheads and lozenge arrowheads with a reserved central zone appear in the Arene Candide Late Neolithic levels. There are also borers and blades retouched to points; the blade sizes are very similar to Chasséen norms. Pottery also shows similarities, including carinated bowls with perforated buttons on the carination, and globular vessels bearing Pan-pipes. A clay 'bille' was also found.

Economic strategy at the Arene Candide site does not seem to alter much in the Late Neolithic levels; the vast majority of faunal remains are of domesticated species (sheep 50%, goat 20%, pig 20%, cattle 10%) (Emiliani, *et al*, 1964, p. 136; fig. 2).

Both Arene Candide and other Ligurian caves (Caverna dei Pipistrelli, Caverna Pollera, Arma del Anime) have produced, in addition to typically Chasséen artifacts, vessel types (such as the flat-based low bowl) and artifacts (for example, kidney-shaped loom weights) more usual in the Po valley Late Neolithic.

The Po valley Late Neolithic is the name given by Guerreschi, publisher of the type-site material, to the culture previously labelled Lagozza (Guerreschi, 1967). A number of dates have been produced for material from the village of Lagozza di Besnate. A pile or wooden post from recent excavations has been dated variously by different Italian laboratories – 3030 b.c., 2630 b.c., 2785 b.c. (R–338, 78a, 78) and $2844 \pm 90$ (Pi–34). An old find of a wooden 'boomerang' was dated $2855 \pm 50$ b.c. (R–337).

It seems, therefore, that this site was occupied towards the beginning of the first half of the third millennium b.c. Pollen analysis suggested that at the time of occupation there existed a lake surrounded by heath, which developed into a rather arid meadow. The surrounding forest was of humid Mediterranean type, with oak dominant (Durante Pasa and Pasa, 1956). Unfortunately no faunal remains were found, probably due to the acidity of the peat, but remains of wheat, barley, and lentils indicate agriculture; flax was also grown, and it has been suggested that the clay discs and kidney-shaped cylinders found at the site were used as spindle-whorls and loom weights respectively. Pears, apples, hazel nuts and acorns were also found at the site. Only a small amount of the chipped and polished stone industry found on the original excavations has been preserved – transverse arrowheads, burins, axes and whetstones. Unusual finds included nine incised pebbles (Figure 18:10), four of which were apparently found together and in the same place as one of the larger groups of loom weights (Guerreschi, 1967, p. 229).

The pottery from the site consists of carinated cups, globular vessels with pierced buttons, truncated jars with bosses all over the surface, low open bowls with flat base, five elaborately brimmed plates, and five lids. One of the plate rims, and four of the lids are decorated (for example, Figure 18:6), and Guerreschi illustrates by macro-photo that simultaneous use was made of wet-incised zigzag lines, seed impressions and a criss-cross pattern etched on a dried or fired surface (Guerreschi, 1967, p. 134). Nearly half the spindle-whorls are also decorated, usually with a rayed pattern, and the site also produced a stone 'anthropomorph' with channelling at right angles to its length (Figure 9:5).

The Lagozza di Besnate assemblage is unique to the type-site, although certain artifacts are known from the caves already mentioned in Liguria, and from other sites in the Po valley like Pescale and Rivoli. At Rivoli in the Eastern Po valley (Barfield, 1966) the majority of finds were of the final Square-Mouthed phase (Rivoli–Castelnuovo) but some Lagozzan artifacts and carbon-14 dates suggest that it was occupied about the same time ($3270 \pm 120$ b.c., $3270 \pm 130$ b.c. – Birm. 103, 104). A fragment of copper was found at this period (Barfield, 1971, p. 49).

Jarman has analysed the fauna from Rivoli, and compared it with the earlier site of Molino Casarotto (Jarman, 1971). Using relative size of the species from site to site as a criterion, he suggests that red deer and pig 'management' at the earlier site gives way to a sheep/goat/cattle/pig economy – still with some red deer – by the mid-third millennium b.c. (Jarman, 1971, p. 262). In his view sheep/goat, not previously native to the region, were introduced about 4500 b.c.

---

*Figure 18. Po valley Late Neolithic (after Guerreschi). Nos. 1–6, pottery (note No. 6, 'lid' decorated by impression and incision); Nos. 7, 8, 9, clay spindle-whorl, loom weights; No. 10, incised pebble.*

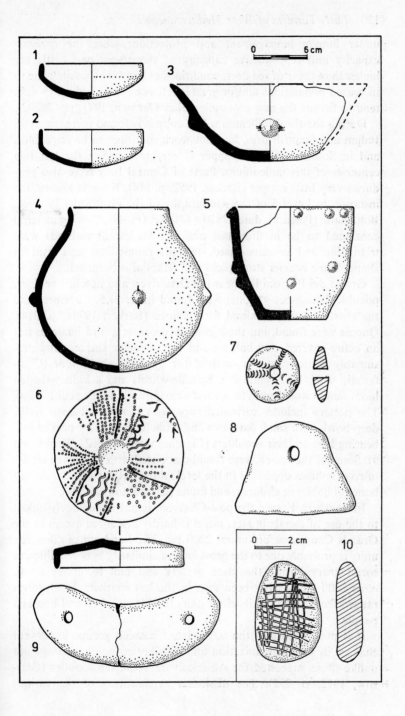

under human management and protection; since the carrying capacity and reproductive capacity of sheep/goat and cattle are higher than those of red deer, conditions of pressure (possibly due to increased populations and/or greater reliance on agriculture) would tend to favour the new economic policy (Jarman, 1971, pp. 262–3).

During the third millennium b.c. copper is found increasingly in Italian and Spanish sites, but flint work continues to be important, and in Southern France copper is very rare before the last two centuries of this millennium. Parts of Central Italy have also produced very little copper (Barker, 1972, p. 114). None is known, for instance, in Level 5 of the stratigraphy of the Grotta dei Piccioni, Bolognano (Pescara), dated 2820 ± 110 b.c. (Pi–49). Cutting material continued to be in flint and obsidian blades; arrowheads were triangular and concave-based, tanged, rhomboidal and oval in shape. Some heavier stone picks and flakes also occurred.

Grotta dei Piccioni lies near the Orta river, and notched pebbles, possible fishing-net weights, were found in Level 5. Caprines were the most important animal food source (Barker, 1974a, p. 214). Querns were found, but these contained ochre; a bird humerus has an ochre-covered clay ball around one articular surface, and presumably demonstrates a method for applying the colour (Cianfarani, *et al,* 1962, plate 86). Spindle-whorls and a kidney-shaped loom weight would seem to suggest weaving and thus flax cultivation. The pottery includes carinated cups with sharply inturned walls, deep bowls with small flat bases and globular jars, some necked and bearing lugs on their shoulders (Cianfarani, *et al,* 1962, plates 8 and 9). Some of the vessels were found associated with the eleven circles of river cobbles deposited in the level; three of the circles contained bones of babies or children, and fauna (Cianfarani, *et al,* 1962, p. 96).

In Southern France the post-Chasséen is not immediately linked to the use of metal; in fact, metal is hardly evidenced except in the Grands Causses before about 2200 b.c. The break-up of Chasséen unity is probably due to the gross lack of similarity between different social groups using the same pottery and flint technique up to *circa* 2500 b.c. As has been seen in the last chapter, these groups ranged from small family-sized units to villages of several hundred people.

It is postulated that the larger late Chasséen groups underwent changes in social organization and possibly economic strategy not unlike those suggested for American Basketmaker societies (Glassow, 1972, p. 272). The dissimilar organization of the various

Chasséen communities would place considerable stress on the mechanism which linked them together, and it actually broke down.

At about the same time the collective burial cult seems to have spread to Southern France, which contains half of all French megaliths (Clottes, 1970, p. 65). In addition, plain menhirs and statue-menhirs are widely found. There are published descriptions of many of the megalithic tombs (for example, Daniel, 1960; Arnal, 1963; Clottes, 1969). The same regional specialities occur as in other countries covered by the same cult; in the Lot department and surrounding area (Quercy) most of the over 500 megalithic tombs are simple rectangular chambers, some of them with a passage, covered by a round tumulus. Grave-goods include masses of beads, with the later graves containing copper ones. Approximately 70 plain menhirs seem to have been erected about the same time.

In the Aude department 'gallery graves' occur. On the Grands Causses a very vigorous school of stone-workers produced nearly 600 megalithic tombs (for example, Plate 3) and over thirty statue-menhirs. Statue-menhirs are large blocks of stone sculpted to some degree of resemblance to the human form. Arnal *et al* have described the Aveyron group as being mostly masculine, decorated across the chest with an elongated pointed pendant (Arnal, *et al,* 1966). Sometimes this design is later removed and breasts added, so that the statue is feminized. Faces, arms, 'cloaks' and 'girdles' can often be distinguished. The Gard group have a characteristically small owl-like head and lines of channelling at each side (Hugues and Jeantet, 1967, and Plate 5). Statue-menhirs are rarely recovered *in situ,* but some have been found in funerary contexts, associated with graves, megalithic and rock-cut tombs (Guilaine, 1968, p. 170; Arnal, *et al,* 1966; Gagnière and Granier, 1967). Two were reused at the Lébous (Hérault) settlement.

Megalithic tombs are naturally missing from the Garonne valley, where Chasséen artifacts may have lingered on after 2500 b.c. A hut floor at Grépiac produced both Chasséen and Late Neolithic pottery, including a deep cylindrical jar with channelling below the rim (Méroc, 1959, fig. 10). Late Neolithic pottery is also known from Le Verdier, but the finds here result from collections rather than excavations. It is in the Lot department that the nearest stratigraphies are available to detail the post-Chasséen development. For instance, at the site of La Perte du Cros, Saillac, the Chasséen assemblage evolved during Level II, losing incised decoration and the multi-perforated lug by the beginning of Level I, and increasing the use of cordons and channelling (Galan, 1967, fig. 35). The date for the beginning of Level I is given as 2600 b.c. (Heidelberg). Well-made, burnished globular vessels with round and flat bases, sometimes decorated with cordons forming a shoulder, are found in Level I together with flat-based deeper jars and a few carinated bowls. One little low bowl contained Emmer and *Triticum compactum*. The very small lithic industry at this site is represented by transverse arrowheads on flakes in Level II but only a few flakes in Level I. Two of the 'billes' or stone balls commonly associated with the Chasséen are also found in Level I (Galan, 1967, p. 30). Faunal analysis revealed that cattle and pig formed the predominant part of the meat source, followed by much smaller percentages of red and roe deer (cattle 44·4%, pig 37·0%, red deer 11·2%, roe deer 7·4% – Ducos *in* Galan, 1967, p. 69).

In the Rhône delta rock-cut tombs, a local school of statue-menhir sculpture, and Languedocian, Courronien and Epi-Chasséen elements seem to indicate the presence of an edge-zone, its other perimeter being the Epi-Chasséen of Haute Provence. A similar flurry of activity is seen on the far Western borders of Languedoc, where local pottery styles are found in the region of St Pons and Véraza. In Languedoc itself an important new culture develops, the Ferrières.

The area around St. Pons, Western Hérault, contains material relatable to the terminal Neolithic of South-Western France; to the first 'Chalcolithic' of the Grands Causses; and to the Ferrières culture in the Hérault-Gard-Ardèche departments. In addition a local speciality in ceramic design develops – a deep squat jar with an encircling plain cordon, which expands into a lug at four points. An assymetrical arrowhead is also locally typical (Rodriguez, 1968). The Saintponien Late Neolithic is represented at the Grotte de Labeil, Laurox (Hérault) where a Chasséen assemblage in Level 9 is replaced in Level 8 by some carinated bowls of Chasséen type, but also plastic pastilles, cordons swelling into lugs, and a roughly hatched triangle scratched below the rim of a deep bowl (Bousquet, Gourdiole and Guiraud 1966, fig. 60). Of nine arrowheads in this level, four are assymetrical; among the blades is one in obsidian (Bousquet, Gourdiole and Guiraud 1966, fig. 66.16). Levels 7 and 6 at the same site continue to produce sherds decorated with cordons and pastilles and hatched triangles, and add chevron incision in the Ferrières style.

The high numbers of basalt querns found in the post-Chasséen levels at this site suggest a continued dependence on agriculture. Animal bones in Levels 8 and 7 are limited to the species of sheep, red deer and boar, but in Level 6 goat and cattle are added to the list. Red deer antler is used for borers and for antler sleeves, of the cylindrical and winged varieties; this increased use of antler as a raw material is typical of the Saintponien Late Neolithic.

The date for this development can be fixed fairly well from carbon-14 dates for other sites; at St Etienne-de-Gourgas not far from Labeil, the excavator found assymetrically shaped arrowheads in all levels (Arnal, G. B., 1970), but the mixture of carinations and jars with smooth cordons only occurred in Hearths 16 to 18, which must be immediately posterior to Hearths 19 and 22, dated 2600 b.c. Rodriguez's Camprafaud cave site, Ferrières-Poussarou, contains in Level 10, dated $2400 \pm 140$ b.c. (Gif 1157), one carinated bowl, but mainly cordoned wares, and an assymetrical arrowhead.

An interesting open-air site of this culture has recently been found at Dorio, Félines-Minervois (Arnal and Rodriguez, 1971). Nine hut floors, rectangular in shape and with large posts at their corners, ranged in size from Hut 1, 5 m × 2·40 m to Hut 5, 8 m × 2·80 m. Hearths were visible in the South-East angle of Huts 1 and 2, and in the North-West angle of Hut 9. In this case there were no carinated jars, but the deep provision jars with superimposed cordons closely resemble Ferrières ones (Arnal and Rodriguez, 1971, fig. 5.1), and the typical lugs were found protruding from single cordons. Antler points and used tines were found. The polished axes have been examined by Tamain, who concludes that the raw material for their production could have been obtained within a radius of 20 km (Tamain *in* Arnal and Rodriguez, 1971).

The Ferrières culture is located mainly in the present-day departments of Hérault, Gard and Ardèche. In Hérault assemblages of this culture are found in forty living sites (seven of them open-air) and six megalithic tombs: in Gard there are thirty-eight sites (nine open-air) and four megalithic tombs, and in Ardèche twenty sites (three open-air) with such assemblages. These figures are taken from a table by Arnal, *et al*, (1967); they omit questionable sites, but include seven sites added by the author from inspection of collections in the Nîmes Natural History Museum.

The number of cave sites is very high, especially when the Chasséen settlement pattern in the same area is considered. In Hérault fourteen sites have produced Chasséen assemblages (nine of them open-air); in Gard twenty-three sites are known to date from the

Chasséen (eleven of them open-air); and in Ardèche only three sites are known to have been occupied at this period, all caves. There are thus a number of contrasts: firstly, an overall increase in sites in Gard-Hérault from the Chasséen to the Ferrières (particularly remarkable – 78 : 37 – when the long Chasséen of at least a thousand years is compared to the two- or three-hundred-year duration of the Ferrières). Secondly, both an absolute and a proportional drop in the number of open-air sites occurred. Thirdly, a change in site location was made, from the two main loci of Chasséen occupation (around the Montpellier area and in the Gardon valley), to the limestone plateau to the North and West of Montpellier (Smith, 1972; Arnal, *et al,* 1967, fig. 17), including the edge of the Causse of Blandas, the area between Uzès and Alès and the department of Ardèche between Ruoms and Les Vans. This expansion into the Ardèche also contrasts markedly with the limited Chasséen penetration; however, the Chasséen was much better represented in the Bouches-du-Rhône and Aveyron, into which a little Ferrières material penetrates. The move from the Hérault lagoon-side in the Late Neolithic has been commented upon by Prades, who confirms that there was a continued use of the lagoon edge in the Late Neolithic, but that many more sites were established in the interior than in earlier centuries (Prades, *et al,* 1967, p. 27).

Very few Ferrières sites have been thoroughly published, but good stratigraphies are available from two caves on the peripheries of the Ferrières area, Grotte de Labeil in Hérault (Bosquet, Gourdiole and Guiraud, 1966) and Grotte de Peyroche II in Ardèche (Roudil and Saumade, 1968). The Grotte des Pins, Blandas (Gard) has a Ferrières level dated $2400 \pm 130$ b.c. (Gif 1360).

An open-air site, Beaussement, Chauzon (Ardèche) lies on the limestone plateau above the Ardèche, and covers several thousand square metres (Montjardin, 1962, p. 15). The soil has now vanished from the surface of the plateau, though shrubs grow tenaciously in the faults between the limestone blocks. Into one of these faults had been deposited successive layers of Ferrières and later material. Ferrières decorations include the incised chevron, parallel incised lines lying horizontally below the rim, and sometimes vertically below buttons; pastilles pushed out from inside the vase, or added; cordons; and sherds with painted decoration below the rim (Montjardin, 1965, p. 32) (*see* Figures 20:1, 3). Carbon-14 dates of 2220 b.c. (Gif 246) and 2150 b.c. (Gif 245) have been obtained from the Ferrières level.

The faunal analysis for this level indicated nearly equal numbers of sheep and cattle, plus slightly fewer pig, and about 5% goat (Poulain-Josien, 1965). Bones of domesticated animals belong to a minimum of 34 individuals, and represent about 85% of the total fauna recovered. Red deer, boar, badger and rabbit were hunted, and two dogs identified.

If meat weight values are calculated for the individual animals belonging to different species, the cattle must have provided approximately 900 kg of edible meat, as against 200 kg and 300 kg respectively from sheep and pig. These are only very approximate figures, but are relevant to comments made below about Late Neolithic economies in Languedoc and neighbouring zones.

Few details are available regarding Late Neolithic economy on the Grands Causses, although sheep and cattle are represented in deposits, and grains of wheat and barley were found throughout the Late Neolithic levels at Sargel I (Balsan and Costantini, 1972, p. 247). This site produced post-Chasséen levels which have enabled Costantini to distinguish two phases of the 'Causses Chalcolithic' (Costantini, 1970, p. 97). Fragments of copper awls and blades are found; leaf and tanged arrowheads in pink or beige chert dominate the earlier phase and crenelated arrowheads the later. There are a great variety of bead types. In the earlier phase winged limestone beads, calibrated shell beads, steatite beads, and pendants in dentalium and limestone are found (Costantini, 1967, pp. 744–5; 1970, pp. 95–8, and Plate 4). Similar bead types are illustrated from the Gard tomb of Peyro Blanco, St Julien-les-Rosiers, together with the schist plaque which appears in the later phase (Figure 21). Carbon-14 dates are rare apart from dates of 2650 b.c. at the Les Treilles cave, and 2550±150 b.c. (Gif 444) for Level VI (1965 excavations) at Sargel I.

Most of the beads are found in funerary contexts; at the Les Treilles cave skeletons with trepanned skulls were accompanied by winged beads. Bordreuil has claimed that this bead type is found exclusively in funerary contexts, particularly in the Languedocian passage graves (Bordreuil, 1966). The gradual increase in jewellery items placed with the dead during the second half of the third millennium b.c. may reflect a basically egalitarian society with acquired status indicated by ornaments or amulets.

Also relying on the Sargel I stratigraphy, Lorblanchet has underlined the essential continuity from the Chasséen into the Late Neolithic or Chalcolithic of the Grands Causses (Lorblanchet,

1970, pp. 102–3). He dates the early post-Chasséen *circa* 2600–2500 b.c. to *circa* 2300–2200 b.c. on the Southern Causses, and the later phase, the Rodezien of Costantini, to the following centuries, over the Northern Causses as well.

Most Rodezien finds come from collective burials in megalithic tombs, either as primary or secondary deposits. The winged bead vanishes, but centrally expanded white limestone beads, biconical copper beads, crenelated arrowheads and polished back flint daggers (similar to that from Peyro Blanco shown in Figure 21:9) are found in Rodezien assemblages. The presence of some artifacts in bronze suggests that the final Rodeziens were contemporary with the beginning of the Bronze Age.

Copper metallurgy on the Causses may be linked with the copper sources of the region, for instance the ore available ten kilometres to the South of the Treilles cave (Costantini, 1970, p. 126). The blade from Sargel I, Level X has been analysed to prove that it contains pure copper plus traces of nickel and silver (Junghans 21, 307). Copper slag has been found in Level 9 at Camprafaud (2350 ± b.c.) and a fragment of copper awl at St Etienne-de-Gourgas *circa* 2300 b.c. (Guilaine, 1970a, p. 126).

The Rhône delta seems to have been an edge area in the second half of the third millennium. There is one case of stratified occupation at the open-air village of Collet-Redon, La Couronne, on a limestone plateau one and a half kilometres from the Mediterranean sea. Here a site stretching over three hectares, partially limited by a heavy wall, has a Bell Beaker house overlying the first, 'Couronnien', occupation (Gagnière, 1963, p. 349). The Couronnien occupation is dated 2400 b.c. (Escalon de Fonton, 1971). One house has been completely excavated, and consists of a substantial main wall twenty metres long running North–South, made of stones mortared together with heavy clay. The house had two chimneys, and its Eastern wall is represented by a line of post-holes 2·5 to 6 m away from the mortared wall. The chimneys were of clay covered in basketry and reached above the height of the thatched roof (Escalon de Fonton, 1971). Many sheep bones were found in hearths and dumps (Gagnière, 1961, pp. 368–70), and during the exploration of the area to the West of the house a magazine area was found with a row of storage vases up to 80 cm in height each decorated with four large lugs, containing bones, and in one case a complete skeleton of a sheep. Obviously this animal was an important food source, but cattle, fish, shell-fish and occasional game were consumed; Escalon de Fonton has stated that a 1000 m² 'kraal' existed (Escalon de Fonton, 1971). The abundance of querns and sickle stones seems to indicate the importance of agriculture also.

Only interim publications have been made about the La Couronne village, and the only pottery types known apart from the big storage jars are hemispherical and subspherical bowls, decorated with saddle lugs, 'bobbin' lugs or small vertical cordons. The lithic industry contains heavy flakes with steep side retouch (often on banded flint), piercing arrowheads, heavy scrapers on flakes, greenstone axes and chisels, and tiny serpentine beads. Pendants are also known in bone and shell. Spindle-whorls may represent wool spinning.

The Courronien assemblage forms part of the polythetic Rhône valley culture of the last half of the third millennium.

This culture is represented in both open-air sites (for example, Estoublon, Eygalières, La Balance-Avignon) and caves (for example, Baume des Enfers, Grotte Basse, both in the commune of Cheval-Blanc). It is also known from rock-cut tombs (for example, Perpétiari, Roaix, Fontvieille) and from flint-making areas (for example, Murs, Malaucène, Châteauneuf-du-Pape). The statue-menhirs of the Rhône valley (Gagnière and Granier, 1963; 1967) probably belong to this culture.

As has been stated, the hallmark of a polythetic culture is that not all its elements are found at any one site, although a majority are found at each site. The Rhône valley late Neolithic ceramics seem to be mainly of the bowl or cylindrical jar type. Plastic additions include plain cordons occasionally superimposed, and a variety of lugs (saddle, tunnel, bilobed, pierced), plus pastilles. Incision in the Ferrières style and channelling in the Fontbouïsse style is known, as are Bell Beaker pots in both International and Provençal styles (Gagnière, 1968, pp. 493–4). Spindle-whorls, often with incised decoration, are also made of baked clay.

On the lithic side, the Rhône valley Late Neolithic uses large blades with steep retouch or no retouch at all; arrowheads are usually either completely or nearly completely retouched bifacially, in leaf or lozenge shapes, and the tanged-and-barbed arrowhead is also known. Frontal and side scrapers are made on flakes. The copper awl of square cross-section or with central expansion is also typical.

As with other Late Neolithic assemblages, the Rhône valley Late Neolithic makes use of varied pendants and beads. Pierced long-bones and shells, pierced boar's tusk and bone pendants in the hook shape, are all found. Limestone rings, and beads in limestone, steatite and other stones are also typical.

Incised, channelled and Bell Beaker wares seem to have been contemporaneous at the settlement site dug as a rescue operation at Quartier de la Balance, Avignon (Gagnière, 1966; 1968; 1970). A carbon-14 date of 2155 ± 120 b.c. was obtained for the assemblage. A fragment of a small statue-menhir had been reused on this site (Gagnière and Granier, 1963, fig. 25). It has the elongated, square-ended nose, and straight 'hair' line of other Rhône valley statue-menhirs (Figure 19), and is small like them, but its round head and lack of chevron incised 'hair' are distinctive, as is the series of cupulae which decorate the back of the head, and the lower face in the form of a sun centre (Figure 19:3). The faunal material from this site includes small cattle, sheep, horse, boar, red and roe deer, fox, dog, badger and wildcat. The horse thus makes an appearance contemporary with that in Lot sites. The fauna suggests the Avignon plain was wooded at the time (Gagnière, 1966, p. 585). Apart from their meat supply, the occupants of La Balance at Avignon probably grew domesticated plants, as the site has also produced many limestone querns.

The rock-cut tombs of the commune of Fontvieille, thirty kilometres South of Avignon, have been claimed to belong to the Chasséen period (Arnal, Latour and Riquet, 1953, pp. 58–9), but have produced material mostly ascribable to the Rhône valley Late Neolithic, such as pottery with channelling or heavy lugs or with an umbilical base. The tombs are cut into Tertiary sandstone or limestone, and covered with capstones. Coutinargues is exceptional in that a trench was dug to accommodate a dry-stone walled structure with megalithic stones forming a short end and a central barrier. An anthropomorphic stela three metres high is reputed to have come from near this tomb (Constans, 1921, p. 17). The finely worked leaf and lozenge arrowheads with semi or totally invasive flat bifacial retouch, found at Coutinargues, La Source and Bounias (Figures 22:1–9) have always been comparable to the equally

---

*Figure 19. Statue-menhirs of Provence (after Gagnière and Granier). No. 1, Lauris (Vaucluse); Nos. 2, 4, 5 Organ-Senas (Bouches-du-Rhône); No. 3, Avignon, Rocher des Doms (Vaucluse). Height: No. 1, 32 cm; No. 2, 28 cm; No. 3, 26 cm; No. 4, 30 cm, remaining; No. 5, 30 cm.*

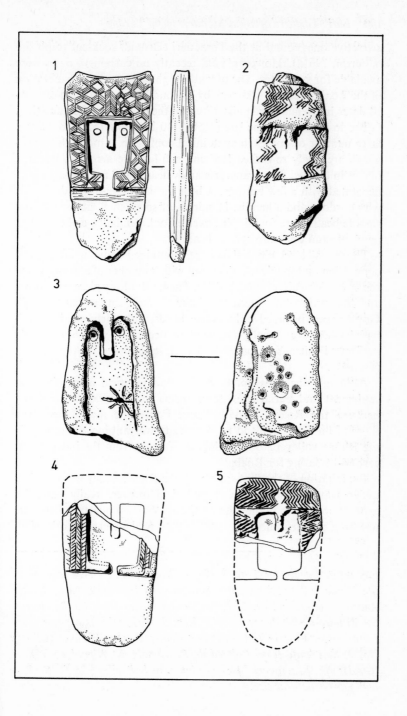

attractive ones found at the Perpétiari (Drôme) rock-cut tomb site (Courtin, 1961a). However, until recently no carbon-14 dates were available for such sites. The breakthrough came with the excavation of the Roaix rock-cut tomb site by J. Courtin, who obtained carbon-14 dates in the late third millennium for the two levels of inhumation.

The lower level of the site (2150 ± 140 b.c., Gif 1620) contains a large number of bodies in anatomical confusion. Among the grave-goods are finely reworked leaf and sub-lozenge arrowheads, large blades in banded flint, transverse arrowheads, and round-based pots decorated with a few buttons. A little flat-based vase was decorated with cordons and a handle. Hundreds of small shell, limestone, and steatite beads were found, plus twelve hook pendants, eight trilobed pendants and one pure copper bead.

The second level of burials (Plate 6) contained bodies in anatomical connection on top of each other, but with a number of arrowheads in the bones (Gagnière, 1968, p. 501). These were long piercing arrows, and the burials have been suggested to represent a 'battle level'. Grave-goods included only twelve beads, but thirty small round-based vases, occasionally carinated or decorated with horizontally perforated buttons or pastilles. This level is dated 2090 ± 140 b.c. (Gif 857).

Although one does not expect to find identical assemblages at settlement and burial sites, there seems to be sufficient similarity between the Roaix, Perpétiari and Fontvieille assemblages and those of La Couronne and La Balance to warrant including them in the Rhône valley Late Neolithic, even apart from the independent carbon-14 dating for Roaix.

Exploitation of the flint sources of the Rhône valley was certainly under way in the Chasséen period. However, really extensive exploitation began in the Late Neolithic. Waisted quartzite hammers weighing over ten kilograms are found at Malaucène and other flint

---

*Figure 20. Languedoc Late Neolithic. Nos. 1, 3, Ferrières vases from Station de la Jasse des Boeufs, Sanilhac and Hirondelle cave, Sainte-Anastasie (Gard); Nos. 4, 7, Fontbouïsse vases from La Rouquette, Ste Hilaire-de-Brethmas (Gard); Nos. 5, 6, Fontbouïsse vases from Fontbouïsse, Villevieille (Gard) and Grotte Payan, Bouquet (Gard); No. 2, flint knife from Dolmen de Rascassols, St Hippolyte-du-Fort (Gard); No. 8, retouched plaque flint from Salinelles (Gard). Scale – one-quarter natural size.*

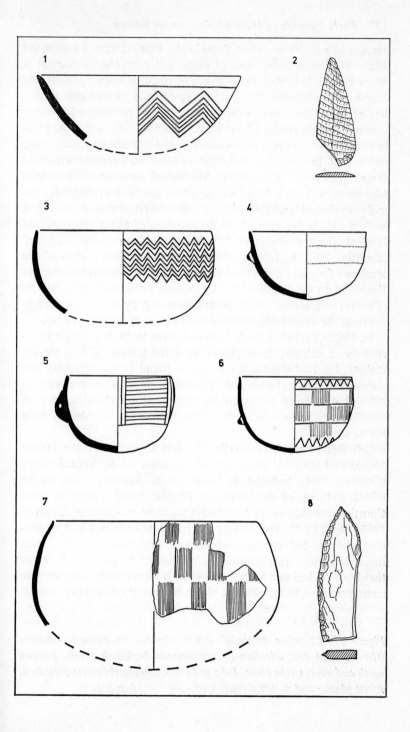

sources like Châteauneuf-du-Pape in the Central Rhône valley and Murs on the Southern slopes of Mont Ventoux. The flint occurs at Murs and Malaucène in long screes of nodules, round or oval, the length of the hillside. Excavations by Schmid proved that miners had exploited the flint to a depth of six metres, possibly using fire as well as stone hammers to extract it (Schmid, 1960; 1963). At Châteauneuf-du-Pape the nodules occur over a low hill now under vine cultivation. In the Avignon Prehistory Museum bifacially retouched large arrowheads and tanged-and-barbed arrowheads from the Murs area seem to indicate a date within the Late Neolithic for the major exploitation of these sites. Courtin has described a number of surface sites in the area of the flint sources of Mont Ventoux, and labelled their assemblages 'Chalcolithic of Chasséen tradition' (Courtin, 1962, p. 14). In another article he gives a map of the location of waisted hammers, indicating smaller flint exploitations at Esperelles to the South of the Lagoon de Berre, and at Eygalières (Courtin and Masse, 1967). Such hammers may have been used to excavate the Fontvieille rock-cut tombs (Constans, 1921, p. 16).

In Upper Provence there does not seem to be any major interruption in cultural development until the advent of Bell Beaker makers. Evolved Chasséen material is found in the relatively low numbers of round chamber and passage graves of Provence, and the cultural continuity seems to be reinforced by the discovery of obsidian arrowheads in a megalithic tomb that has already been mentioned.

Bell Beaker material overlies the last Chasséen at the Grotte Murée and the Abri du Jardin du Capitaine in the Verdon valley (Courtin, 1974), and also at Fontbrégoua, Salernes (Var). In the middle network of the Grotte de l'Eglise, Level 3 contains what Courtin describes as an 'Evolved Chasséen' assemblage (Courtin, 1967a, pp. 283–8). The pottery continued its carinated and shouldered shapes, but cordons were more important, together with indented rims. Lithic materials were similar to previous levels in that lozenge, leaf and tanged arrowheads were found, together with transverse ones, but some thick blades bore steep retouch in much the

*Figure 21. Chamber tomb of Peyro Blanco, St Julien-les-Rosiers (Gard). Plan and selection of grave-goods including beads, pierced tooth and copper ring (Nos. 1–7; note No. 5, winged bead); Nos. 8, 9, schist plaque and polished-back knife-dagger (after Salles).*

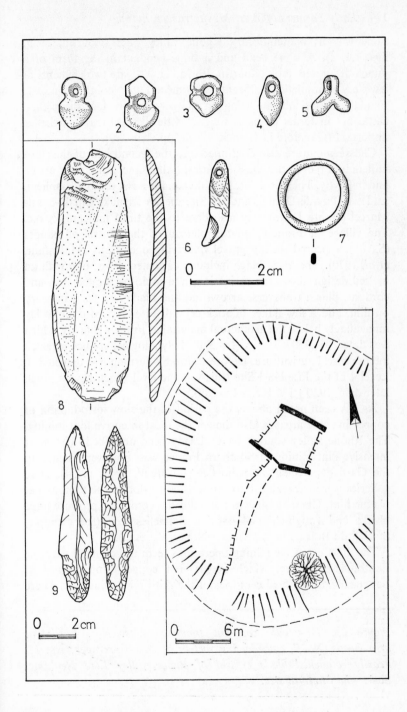

1  2  3  4  5

6  7

0  2 cm

8

9

0  2 cm

0  6 m

same way as contemporary Rhône valley ones (Courtin, 1959, figs. 1.5, 4). A bone bead and a bone pendant in the form of a punch-decorated hook (Courtin, 1967a, fig. 4.8), are two elements of jewellery or amuletic significance at home in Late Neolithic contexts. Faunal remains indicate a higher number of individual sheep than cattle but in terms of meat weight cattle were probably twice as important (Gagnière in Courtin 1967a, pp. 299–300).

Chasséen culture also continued into the second half of the third millennium b.c. in the Massif Central (Allier and Loire river areas) and in Savoy. There is a date of 2100 b.c. for a cist tomb at Banleau, Ludesse (Puy-de-Dôme), and the site of Les Rivaux, Espaly-Saint-Marcel (Haute Loire) may also date to the third millennium b.c. The village of Francin, on the plateau of the Massif of Bauges (Savoy), appeared during gravel quarrying operations (Malenfant, *et al,* 1970). The assemblage included carinated vases, one with an incised design above the carination, and multi-perforated lugs and cordons, plus a transverse arrowhead and blade and flake industry on flint, and a few flakes of rock crystal. Fire-cracked cobbles lay immediately below the artifactual material at Francin Site III, which was dated to $2350 \pm 75$ b.c. (Lv–390). Palynological studies revealed intense cereal agriculture. Deforestation by burning was detected in Level 4 of the Francin I Site (this was the level which gave a much later date, $1920 \pm 170$ b.c. – Lv–389).

As has been noted above, the period of the slow introduction of copper in some areas is also that of the most intensive flint mining. The Rhône valley sources have already been described. The most intensive flint mining of Southern France was, however, located in the Gard department at Salinelles (Bordreuil, 1974, p. 34). Here galleries were excavated into the hillside to obtain the famous flat plaque flint. Open-air sites in the Salinelles commune produce huge blocks and rough-chipped axes of Salinelles flint (for example, Station du Bois de la Rouvière – Nîmes Museum).

The most extensive mining operations seem to be linked with the Fontbouïsse culture, which is the first copper-using culture of Languedoc, in the final centuries of the third millennium b.c. There

*Figure 22. Fontvieille rock-cut tomb contents. Nos. 1–9, flint arrowheads (No. 7, embedded in vertebra); No. 10, scraper; No. 11, heavily retouched blade typical of Rhône valley Late Neolithic. Scale – half natural size.*

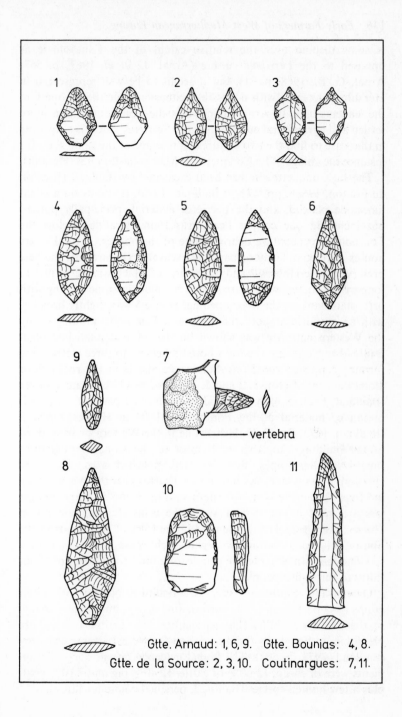

vertebra

Gtte. Arnaud: 1, 6, 9.   Gtte. Bounias:  4, 8.
Gtte. de la Source: 2, 3, 10.   Coutinargues:  7, 11.

is some dispute over the relative extent of the Fontbouïsse as opposed to the Ferrières culture (Arnal, J., *et al,* 1967, p. 567; Arnal, G. B., 1968, p. 81), but it seems to be well represented in Hérault and Gard, with a possible extension over the Rhône into the Vaucluse. G. B. Arnal claims that the Fontbouïsse is a more settled and agricultural culture than the Ferrières, but it is surprising in that case to find the two cultures represented at the same sites, for instance the village of La Conquette, St Martin-de-Londres (Hérault).

The La Conquette site has been excavated by Bailloud (Escalon de Fonton, 1968b, pp. 472–5; Bailloud, 1973). It stands on a slight limestone plateau, and the Ferrières material, principally pottery but including one copper bead, was found stratified below the Fontbouïsse occupation debris in one of the houses. A total of six houses were completely or partially excavated (Figure 23); the best preserved were Houses 2 and 5, the first of which was 12·50 metres long by 3–4 metres wide, surrounded by thick drystone walling with orthostats flanking the door opening. House 5 was slightly broader, with an entrance at both the West and East ends, although only the Western entrance was shown on the original published plan. Bailloud suggests that the walls bore timbers up to three metres long forming a pitched roof; post-holes were visible in the rocky floor along the axes of Houses 2 and 5. The roof would be thatched over (Bailloud, 1973, p. 499). Bailloud has published plans of the distribution of material at the Fontbouïsse level in Houses 2 and 5 (Bailloud, 1973, figs. 2–6). Hearths lie in the Western or back third of the buildings, together with most of the stone manufactures (nuclei, hammerstones, flint industry, polished axes, and river cobbles). Most pottery lies beyond the hearths near the Western wall in House 2 and the North-Western wall in House 5. Large storage jars are most usually found along the walls. Faunal remains in House 5 were very strongly centred in the North Central part of the house. This leads Bailloud to regard each house as the home of a separate family averaging five people, or a total community of about thirty to thirty-five people.

Querns and grindstones suggest agriculture, but no carbonized grains have been found. The surrounding area is under vines today, so there is a possibility that agriculture was feasible in the Late Neolithic, although Bailloud seems to favour a pastoral economy (Bailloud, 1973, p. 504). The faunal evidence reveals 55% of fragments were of sheep, 13·60% of cattle, 12·40% pig and 7·10% goat, plus a few hunted species (Bailloud, personal communication).

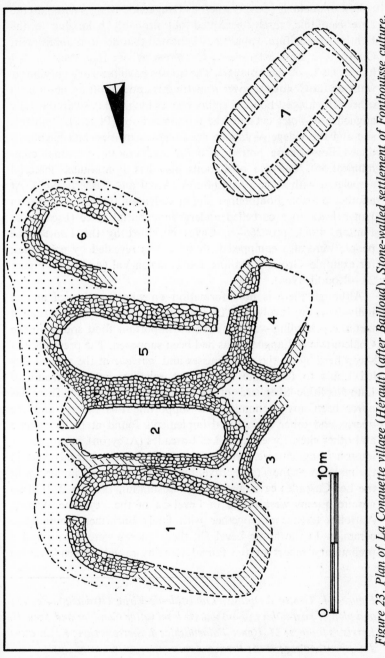

*Figure 23. Plan of La Conquette village (Hérault) (after Bailloud). Stone-walled settlement of Fontbouïsse culture.*

La Conquette is one of numerous Languedoc villages dating to the Late Neolithic, rarely excavated but probably belonging to the Fontbouïsse culture. Roudil has indicated that about a dozen exist. One of the most extensive is Cambous, where four units of 3–4 houses lie 25–60 metres apart. The houses have the same curvilinear walls as La Conquette, over a metre thick and abutting on to each other. The longest house is eighty metres long and has two centrally aligned post-holes cut into the limestone floor (Plate 7). Both this site and the village of Janucq are under excavation and have produced Fontbouïsse pottery (Roudil and Vincent, personal communication). The site of Lébous also has Fontbouïsse material associated with some of its houses (Arnal and Robert, 1967). At another possible Fontbouïsse site at Calvisson (Gard) a passage in Hut 2 leads to a corbelled underground burial place (Escalon de Fonton, 1963, pp. 266–9). Caves occupied by the Fontbouïsse people were also equipped with structures revealed by post-holes, for example Grotte d'Oullins, Labastide-en-Val (Ardèche) (Figure 24 – Roudil, 1966).

Although there is no information on what number of animal individuals are involved at La Conquette, it seems possible that in fact sheep herding was not such an important food source in the Chalcolithic of Languedoc as had been supposed. The prevalence of sheep herding on the arid Causses and *garrigue* at the present day led Louis to formulate his famous economo-cultural group of Late Neolithic 'Shepherds of the Plateaux' (Louis, 1948). There has never been any economic data supporting this theory, and the querns and other agricultural implements found at La Conquette and other sites, for example Les Cascades (Aveyron), suggest some interest in agriculture. On the Grands Causses, ovicaprids were in the majority at the Treilles cave, but cattle were more important at the Les Cascades cave (Balsan and Costantini, 1972, p. 247). Two granite querns were found in Level 5a of the Peyroche II cave, Auriolles (Ardèche), together with finely burnished Fontbouïsse ceramics. In the lower Level 5b, three querns were found, and a preliminary report of the faunal remains reveals dependence on

*Figure 24. Grotte d'Oullins, Labastide-de-Virac (Ardèche). Section and plan of post-holes in Fontbouïsse level (after Combier and Roudil). Levels as follows: M, Upper Palaeolithic; L,Sauveterrian; K, Cardial; J–C, Fontbouïsse; B–A, Bronze Age.*

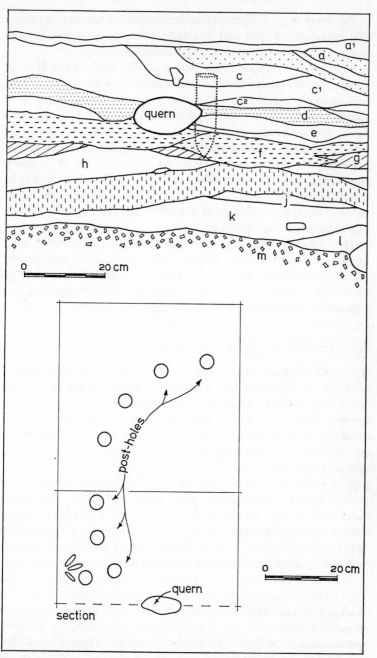

a¹
a
c
c¹
c²
d
e
quern
f
g
h
j
k
l
m

0    20 cm

post-holes

0    20 cm

quern

section

cattle, sheep, goat, dog, considerable numbers of boar, red deer, roe deer and hare (Roudil and Saumade, 1968, p. 164). The authors regard this as a mixed agricultural-pastoral economy.

The faunal remains at four Late Neolithic sites in the Hérault studied by Madame Poulain-Josien (three open-air and one cave site), suggest that in fact cattle were the most important food source (Poulain-Josien, 1957a; 1957b). Even at the La Bergerie Haute site, where the sheep individuals rise to sixteen as against six cattle and four pig, the relevant meat weights of these species (average 20 kg, 90 kg, and 40 kg respectively – Phillips, 1972, p. 44), suggest that approximately 550 kg of meat were being obtained from cattle, 330 kg from sheep and 150 kg from pig. The relative importance of cattle is even higher at two other sites (La Paillade, Grabels and Anis-2-Hortus, Vauflanès).

The different settlement patterns of the Chasséen and later cultures probably reflects differing emphases on agriculture and pastoralism. As has been shown, however, there was a variety of economic modes in both periods, and no single explanation can account for the change in site distribution.

MEGALITHS AND COLLECTIVE BURIAL

The third millennium b.c. is the age of the megalithic tomb. Several thousand of them are found in Iberia, mostly in the South and West, dating from before 3000 b.c. to after 2000 b.c. in different regions. In Southern France megalithic and rock-cut tombs seem to have come into vogue after *circa* 2500 b.c. In Corsica and Sardinia also the last half of the millennium sees the vogue of collective burial spreading widely.

The complexities of the Iberian collective tombs (including here built tombs in drystone and/or great stones, and rock-cut chambers) have been revealed by the publications of Georg and Vera Leisner (1943; 1956–65). Recently Savory has discussed the different tomb types and grave-goods (Savory 1968, chapters 4–6). Some of these are of a different type than the pit-grave assemblages of Catalonia already discussed. Savory says that in the early megaliths and rock-cut tombs of Alentejo (Portugal) slate plaques engraved with geometric patterns 'were apparently placed with each corpse as a personal amulet' (Savory, 1968, p. 100). A more elaborate series of grave-goods come from later tombs around the Tagus river. Cylindrical 'idols' or small menhirs stand in the passages of tombs, while extraordinary slate and schist 'croziers', huge stone hoes, stone lunulae, stone 'pine-cones', even a replica of sandals in ivory, are among the goods deposited (Leisner and Leisner, 1959–65, lief. 3, plates 150–7). Such elaborate non-utilitarian products either symbolize achieved status in a complex social organization, or perhaps even inherited status in a hierarchically organized society.

An extraordinary tomb at Praia dos Maçãs, Sintra (Alentejo) has a date of $2300 \pm 60$ b.c. (Köln) for a late megalithic passage-grave built in drystone in an earlier rock-cut chamber. Another very similar date ($2210 \pm 110$ b.c. – Heidelberg) has been produced for the archaeological level in the small Eastern chamber (Almagro, 1970).

Fortunately we can get some idea of the sort of societies that dug rock-cut tombs and built long graves and passage-and-chamber graves (the latter are in the majority in Iberia, and may have corbelled ceilings). One of a number of probably contemporary settlement sites has been stratigraphically excavated over a small area, Vila Nova de São Pedro to the North-East of Lisbon. In its lower level, which should date to the first half of the third millennium b.c., this open-air site produced slate plaques and other artifacts found in the Alentejo megaliths. Mixed farming seemed to be indicated from the presence of domesticated animals including horse, and the presence of wheat, barley and beans. A domed potter's kiln revealed technological advance in this sphere. The fortification wall at Vila Nova post-dates this early occupation (Savory, 1968, p. 135). At the possibly contemporary site of Zambujal (Torres Vedras, Portugal) massive towers and walls, at first narrow and high, later reinforced, were constructed as the main fortification (Sangmeister and Schubart, 1972, p. 193). Very possibly the forts and bastioned wall at Los Millares (Almeria) were also built before the mid-third millennium b.c.; a date of $2340 \pm 85$ b.c. (H284/247) was obtained on wood found against the outside of the bastioned wall.

Los Millares was a long-lived settlement, with at least eighty passage-graves in its cemetery, many of them elaborately constructed and revetted (Almagro and Arribas, 1963; Leisner and Leisner, 1943). According to Savory, the earliest type of corbel-roofed grave, Los Millares 40, contained plump low bowls and a bottom-heavy vase related to those of the preceding Almerian culture, and a fragment of copper awl (Savory, 1968, p. 147; Leisner and Leisner, 1943, plate 17.1). A tomb of later type, Los Millares 19, has a radiocarbon date of $2430 \pm 120$ b.c. (KN 72). It was contained in a tumulus ten metres in diameter composed of drystone and sand.

All the passage and chamber construction was in drystone except for three port-hole slabs of slate which interrupt the passage. Niches were found in both the passage and chamber. The 3·50-metre diameter chamber produced few grave-goods on re-examination by Almagro and Arribas, simply a fragment of stone bowl, a *Helix* shell, and a number of sherds of red polished straight-walled jars or deep bowls (Almagro and Arribas, 1963, plate CXI). A tomb of similar construction, Los Millares 5, is shown in Figure 25. This produced a copper saw and bowl decorated in 'ocular' style, plus a decorated phalange 'idol' (not shown). Grave-goods varied from stone axes and bone points and combs to decorated pieces of ivory and copper tools (for example, Tomb 41 – Figures 25:1–8). Other copper tools and weapons (awls, axes, chisels, daggers, halberds and knives) are found elsewhere at Los Millares, and the ivory suggests connections with Africa.

The range and variety of the grave-goods, which go well beyond the utilitarian possessions of the individual, and the considerable population suggested by both the size of the cemetery and the amount of public works undertaken at Los Millares, suggest that the inhabitants of this site were part of a complex society with some strong religious affiliations. Maluquer de Motes has suggested that it may have been based on the extended family and a chiefly organization (Maluquer de Motes, 1972, p. 44).

According to Arribas, quoted by Renfrew (1967), there are twenty-four fortified settlements of the Copper Age. The sudden interlocking complexity of cultural forms is impressive: large settlements with stone-built bastioned walls, courtyards and rectangular or oval houses, are exploiting metal ores (copper, silver and lead), but simultaneously producing non-utilitarian stone and bone manufactures and very fine pottery. Some at least of their dead are being housed in tombs of fine stonework and elegant architectural complexity. Presumably the builders of these settlements were agriculturally based. Renfrew has spoken of them in terms of 'proto-urban' (Renfrew, 1967, p. 284).

The last grave-goods deposited in the Los Millares grave passages are Bell Beakers, fine reddish polished pottery with deeply incised or

---

*Figure 25. Los Millares chamber tombs and contents (after Leisner and Leisner). Nos. 1–8, Tomb 41, plan and contents; Nos. 9–12, Tomb 5, plan and contents.*

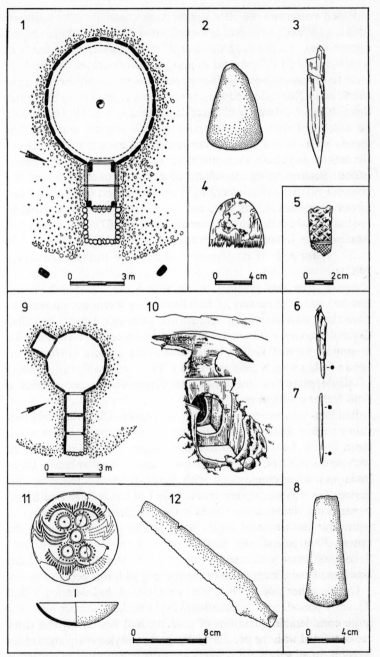

indented patterns. The Bell Beaker vessel, and its accompanying artifacts (archer's wristguard, V-perforated button, gold ornaments, copper axe), are found in the late stages of the stratified levels at Vila Nova de São Pedro and Zambujal. Savory traces Bell Beakers back to the *almagra*-and-incised wares known from the beginning of the Spanish Neolithic, and locates their area of origin on the Central Spanish *meseta*. An early phase of development *circa* 2400 b.c. would be associated with the International Style Beaker, and the later *meseta* styles would occur in the succeeding millennium b.c. Given the lack of good data, there might be justification for the hypothesis of Bell Beakers being manufactured at the fortified sites, and the complex of their traits emerging from this milieu (as Renfrew has already hinted, 1967, p. 282, and as Harrison has emphasized in re-studying the Vila Nova material, 1974, p. 107). The tell site of Almizaraque (Almeria) has produced a date of $2200 \pm 120$ b.c. (KN 73) for a level containing Millares-type Beakers (Almagro, 1962).

Apart from this possible origin within the framework of the fortified sites, the makers of Bell Beakers in Iberia do not seem to have their own individual settlements, although a new site called Cerro de la Virgen (Granada) has produced a series of five dates for a supposedly Bell Beaker house containing a loom ($1970 \pm 35$ to $1850 \pm 35$ b.c. – GrN 5596 and GrN 5764). Presumably the cemetery of single graves on the *meseta* at Ciempozuelos also reflects a Bell Beaker community.

Bell Beakers spread to the Barcelona region, where their relationship to other final third millennium b.c. phenomena is not at all clear. Pericot Garcia claims that the Beakers are usually associated with schist palettes, long blades and transverse arrowheads. Catalonia has some connections with South-Western France at this period, for various pottery types typical of the Véraza and Saintponien Late Neolithic are visible in the Sabadell Museum (deep jars with three superimposed lugs; similar jars with a cordon below the rim swelling periodically into flat lugs). Large blades of banded 'lake flint', often with deep-cutting retouch, and multitudes of flat limestone beads, seem to be contemporary with this period.

On the other side of the Pyrenees, Guilaine has detected a Bell Beaker I period, with International Style Beakers, copper awls and quite considerable quantities of gold. In Bell Beaker III the vases are decorated with the peculiarly 'Pyrenean' styles of zip and ladder incision. In all stages the Beakers are usually deposited in collective tombs, whether megalithic or in caves (Guilaine, 1967). At the rock-shelter of Font-Juvenal, Conques (Aude) a Véraza level is dated 2250 ± 90 b.c. but the overlying Bell Beaker Level is, surprisingly, dated 2450 ± 100 (MC 490–1).

The site of Embusco, Mailhac (Aude) seems to have contained at least two living areas, each of them containing sherds of Bell Beakers and either plain ware or cordoned pots. Southern France has also produced, more recently, a probably 'tented' encampment at St Côme-et-Maruéjols (Hérault), where Roudil has located eighty plain and decorated bowls and jars, all of Bell Beaker inspiration (Roudil, *et al,* 1969).

Treinen has recently described the different regions in which the Beakers are found in France (Treinen, 1970). The West Mediterranean littoral is very rich with eighty-seven sites, including thirty-nine in the Aude alone. The East Mediterranean littoral boasts thirty sites, open-air, burial and cave locations. The La Balance, Avignon (Vaucluse) site, with its mixed assemblage, including Beaker sherds, dated to 2155 ± 120 b.c. (Gif 705), has already been described. Bell Beaker surfaces in the Verdon valley have been dated as follows – Grotte Murée, 2119, 2000 ± 118 b.c. (Gif 116), Abri du Jardin du Capitaine, 2150 ± 140 b.c. (Gif 704). In the Provençal area the Beakers bear comb and incised and stamped designs, and there are more bowls. A few Beakers are found in North Italy, but they are extremely rare in the rest of the peninsula.

In the last half of the third millennium b.c. certain areas of Italy have a well-developed copper metallurgy, such as the Po valley and 'Etruria', where graves of the Remedello and Rinaldone cultures respectively produced axes, awls and daggers. However, this precocious metal-working remained rather closely linked to local ore sources. At the site of La Romita di Asciano, near Pisa (Tuscany), Levels 9, 10 and 11 contain 'Eneolithic' material (Peroni, 1962–3, p. 311). Level 10 of this site has been dated 2298 ± 115 (Pi 100). The Eneolithic levels contained a rather sparse assemblage, with generally poor quality pottery in low bowl, hemispherical and carinated bowl shapes, with troncoconic and inverted vases and necked vases. A fragment of Bell Beaker was found in Level 9. Decoration of the other pottery was by incision or by the addition of smooth cordons and rectangular or vertical nosed lugs. No metal was found in any of the three levels, and flint continued to be used for blades and tanged and lozenge arrowheads. Ground stone was represented by querns and grindstones and a rectangular pendant in limestone.

K

The Central Italian Chalcolithic and Bronze Age has recently been discussed by Barker, who has concluded that there was 'enormous variation in the rates of development and change of the regional Eneolithic and Bronze Age cultures' (Barker, 1972, p. 178). Study of assemblages, faunal samples and evidence of location of sites in this very varied region leads him to the conclusion that 'mobility was probably the dominant component of Neolithic, Eneolithic and Earlier Bronze Age economies, particularly on the Tyrrhenian side of the Apennines' (Barker, 1972, p. 204).

Cazzella, in considering the Eneolithic of Southern Italy and Sicily, has emphasized the lack of lowland sites and also the rarity of faunal samples in Southern Italy. Jarman and Webley believe that the Tavoliere may have continued to be occupied into the Eneolithic, but that a minor climatic change could have made agriculture much less viable. The numerically smaller populations of the Eneolithic probably depended much more on pastoralism than before, so that home bases were established in the Gargano highlands, with less substantial sites on the lowland (Jarman and Webley, 1974, pp. 192–4). Cazzella has pointed out that open-air settlement continues into the Eneolithic in Sicily, where there was apparently less change in economic practice.

South Italy was apparently not penetrated by Bell Beaker makers, and the grave forms of the end of the third millennium b.c. consist mainly of rock-cut tombs (for example, the Gaudo cemetery) and a few megalithic tombs. Copper daggers are found in certain areas, but in general flint and obsidian continue to provide cutting edges in at least the early Eneolithic. Cazzella claims that apart from certain 'closed areas' like the Gaudo an effective trading network developed in Southern Italy during the course of the Eneolithic. Increased improvement of stone working techniques and extension of metallurgy suggest to him a division of labour and a society with leaders to run the longer-range exchanges (Cazzella, 1972, p. 283).

In Malta architectural complexity had reached its height in elaborate temples by the end of the third millennium b.c. The Tarxien Level at the site of Skorba is dated $2430 \pm 150$ b.c. (BM 143), and lasts until *circa* 2000 b.c. according to Trump. The temples are the outcome of the original rock-cut tomb technology and style, carried to extraordinary lengths in the coralline and globigerina limestones of Malta (for example, Evans 1971, plates 6, 10, 15). At Gġantija and Mnajdra quadri and quinlobed temple complexes face on to forecourts (Evans, 1971, plans 38A and 20A respectively).

Renfrew has suggested that pairs or groups of temples controlled areas of arable land, and hypothesizes that about 2000 people would have inhabited each territory (Renfrew, 1973, p. 155).

In Western Corsica Lanfranchi has collected pottery, querns and grindstones, spindle-whorls and arrowheads from a number of open-air sites (for example, Monte Lazzo). Presumably they were occupied by people with an agricultural economy who either grew flax or reared sheep for their wool, during the third millennium b.c. Levels 5 and 6 at rock-shelter 3 of Monte Lazzo were occupied in the Late Neolithic, at which time many rocks with cup-marks are assumed to have been used as querns (Gagnière, 1970, p. 581).

Among the Late Neolithic communities of Corsica megalithic construction may have begun in the first half of the third millennium b.c. (Grosjean, 1971, p. 27). The first period of megalithic building (Grosjean's Megalithic I) involved cists and small menhirs, the standing stones being placed near the burial cists. At first the cists were buried in the ground, but over time they were placed half-way into the ground, and finally stood on the ground surface. Cist cemeteries occur in Southern Corsica at Lévie and Sartène, and often the cist lies at the centre of a ring of stones, not unlike the Sardinian site of Li Muri, Arzachena (Gallura). Grave-goods include necklaces, pierced hammers, and in one case a steatite cup.

During Megalithic II, which lasts until about 1800 b.c., menhirs grew larger, and are found in single or double alignments, for instance at Pagliaiu, Sartène (Grosjean, 1966, plate 17). Megalithic tombs are also built. Remains of red colouration on the standing stones, and the find of a haematite-impregnated mortar at the I Stantare alignment, suggest that many of the menhirs may have been painted (Gagnière, 1970, p. 576; Grosjean, 1971, p. 31).

The second half of the third millennium b.c. on the island of Sardinia sees the passing of the Bonu Ighinu culture, and the beginning of the Sardinian Chalcolithic or Copper Age cultures. Since the amount of copper found is very minimal, and flint and obsidian are widely used, the term Chalcolithic will be used here.

There are two main Chalcolithic cultures in Sardinia, which seem to be geographically isolated from each other (Lilliu, 1972, p. 31). One occurs in North-East Sardinia in the Gallurese district, and seems to have links in funerary type with the nearby South of Corsica. The other is much more widespread over the rest of the island, and is named after the cave of San Michele, Ozieri (Sassari). Lilliu also distinguishes a Bell Beaker culture, but the rare Beakers and associated artifacts have the appearance of individual imports rather than a full assemblage.

The stone rings of the Gallura district with their internal stelae, and sometimes central cists and burials (for example, Li Muri, Arzachena), have produced pottery, flint and polished chisels plus a number of steatite manufactures (a bowl with trumpet lugs, mace-heads and numerous olive-shaped, flat, spheroidal or discoidal beads). Similar assemblages are found in local rock-shelters, some of which seem to have been protected by stone walls (Lilliu, 1972, p. 38), and in about ten megalithic tombs built in the same area.

By contrast the San Michele culture has a much wider distribution on the plains and in the mountains of the rest of the island. Occupation was in caves or open-air villages, and burial in elaborate rock-cut tombs or, occasionally, megalithic tombs. The San Michele level in the Grotta del Guano has been dated $2280 \pm 50$ b.c. (R609). Rock-cut tombs persisted in use for another millennium, and pure levels of San Michele material are rarely found in them. However, some of the more than one thousand rock-cut tombs known in Sardinia (480 of them in the province of Sassari alone) must have been dug out at this time. Lilliu says that they are usually located on poor land, singly or in groups of two or more. Rarely, cemeteries of as many as thirty-six tombs are found (Anghelu Ruju, Alghero). The tombs are excavated into granite or trachite or other rocks, and are amongst the most elaborate of West Mediterranean Europe. The internal details include shaped columns, mock gabling, steps, niches, and alcoves (Ceruti, 1967). Doors are carefully sculpted, and simple designs, frequently stylized bulls' horns, are found above the doorways (for example, Figure 26). Occasionally anthropomorphic figures with arms upraised are carved on the walls (Contu, 1965). Although the earliest deposits in the Santu Pedru Tomb I, Alghero (Sassari) possibly date from just after the end of the third millennium b.c., the tomb is illustrated to give an impression of the complex nature of the architecture (Figure 26) (Contu, 1964). A number of stone picks were found at both Santu Pedru and Anghelu Ruju, and were presumably the tools used for the excavation of the tombs.

The pottery of the San Michele culture has been described by

*Figure 26. Rock-cut tomb of Santu Pedru, Sassari (Sardinia). Isometric drawing of chambers and detail of bull's horn sculpture over entrance to central chamber (after Contu).*

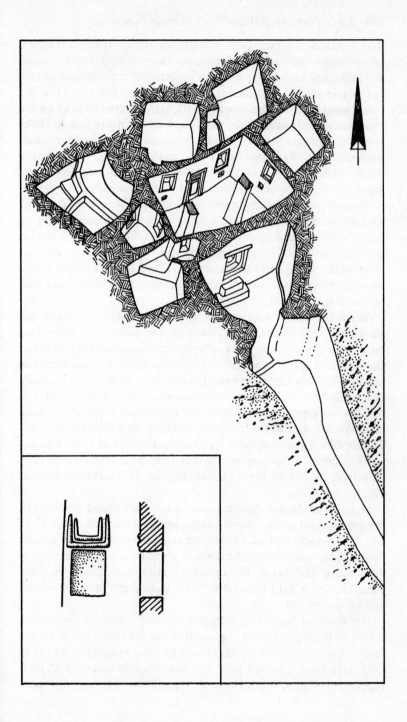

Bray (1963) and Lilliu (1972, pp. 64–77). Apart from plain wares, often tripods, the ceramics are baroque in decoration. Richly incised and impressed vases are so complex in form and decorative attributes as to baffle general description. Bases are usually flat. From this flat base a bowl can have flaring walls, with half-circles of incision on the outer walls, and occasionally also outer base (Grotta San Michele, and Grotta Monte Maiore, Thiesi). A biconical shape is also typical: the walls below the carination are high and deeply incurved above the flat base (for example, Guido, 1963, plate 4). The base, lower and upper wall may be thickly decorated with hatched Vs and horse-shoes, or hatched concentric circles. A deep carinated bowl from the level above the Bonu Ighinu assemblage at Sa Uca bears a row of female figures round its upper wall (Loria, 1971). This site has also produced globular forms, with lugs sunk into the pot side and accentuated by swathes or circles of incised lines. Another extra-ordinary shape is of an inverted flower-pot, with small head and several feet.

Although foreign connections of the San Michele people are shown by the presence of Bell Beakers, and possibly by Salinelles-type plaque flint, and there are elements of similarity between Cycladic and Sardinian idols, or between some Maltese ceramics and San Michele wares, the San Michele culture seems to be basically of local development. The footed vases which play so large a part in Sardinian prehistory persist from the little stubbed feet of the Late Neolithic to become long triangular feet in the San Michele ceramics. The Sardinian rock-cut tomb development attains as great a singu-larity as the contemporary temple architecture on Malta, or the later megalithic tombs of the Balearics (Evans, 1971; Pericot Garcia, 1972).

Material of the San Michele culture has been found stratified in the lowest level of the sloping ramp up to the square 'temple' of Monte d'Accodi, Sassari. Finds from this site on view in the Sassari Museum include hemispherical vases, a small carinated vase decor-ated above and below the carination with horizontally hatched triangles, and a flat plate about 50 cm in diameter with a low wall and out-rolled rim.

The Monte d'Accodi stratigraphy revealed successive occupation dating to the Early Bronze Age, so that the final form of the thirty-metre square, revetted structure and its long ramp (Plate 8) may only have been achieved after the San Michele culture had been superseded (Contu, 1971). However, the site was obviously extremely important, not only from the point of view of this unique mound, but also because of the two menhirs and capstoned cist that are beside the ramp, and the enormous egg-shaped stone that lies some distance away from the end of the ramp. Very large quantities of pottery, obsidian, flint, ground stone and shells have been excavated and are now being analysed in the Sassari Museum. The prevalence of *Helix* both on this site and in the Anghelu Ruju tombs suggest that molluscs were still important in the economy, although it seems likely that the presence of open villages and large numbers of querns denote agriculture as a base for this society. The vast labour involved in works like Monte d'Accodi or the rock-cut tombs, and the professional technique of the San Michele potters, all suggest fairly elaborate social organization, which one would normally associate with an economy of domesticated plants and animals. The elaboration of both the tombs and the 'temple', and the presence of marble schematic figurines in some of the San Michele assemblages, suggests a strong religious element in the society.

The great variety in material culture in the third millennium b.c. contrasts markedly with occupation levels described from preceding periods. Although there is considerable regional and local diversity, a general increase in the types of objects produced by each society can be seen. Since most of the items immediately connected with the food quest had already been produced in the earlier period, most of the new elements are likely to function in other sub-systems of the culture.

A number of features can be isolated: in the first place there must have been an overall increase in population, if we are to account for the increase in numbers of sites. Secondly, there was a change in site location from earlier periods in a number of areas, for instance Languedoc, Southern Italy and parts of Iberia. Thirdly, there seems to have been some change in economic practices, linked possibly to environmental change. Obviously there are links between the changes in site location and in economy and in some stone and pottery types.

Cross-cutting local variation in material culture is the cult of collective burial in a single tomb or in a cemetery. The individual is now absorbed into the group, and buried according to his residential or kinship affiliation. More grave-goods are offered than ever before, and an attempt has been made to suggest that some may reflect a society where high status can be achieved and others one where it may be inherited. The extreme elaboration of some tombs (for example, Los Millares, St Michel-du-Touch) suggests the presence of a chief or ruling clan.

The indication of cemeteries by megalithic structures, stelae, rings of stones, etc., all serve to emphasize the role of the dead as possessors of the surrounding land, and the rights of their successors to it. By the end of the third millennium b.c. competition for various resources – land, minerals, herds – seems to have caused conflict in various areas. Locally based populations (tribes or chiefdoms in anthropological parlance) were establishing their individuality and improving their technological capacity. Up to several hundreds of persons may have been bound together by ties of kinship or sodalities. The majority of public works of West Mediterranean Europe are not elaborate houses, palaces or cities, built by servile labour for a ruling class. They seem rather to represent a communal effort on a considerable scale to build monuments to the dead. From the surviving evidence we can best conclude that West Mediterranean Europeans on the eve of the Bronze Age were involved in a search for prestige for their ancestors and gods.

# 6. Conclusion

Over much of West Mediterranean Europe the outline of Neolithic development is clear in artifact and assemblage terms, and is temporally controlled by radiocarbon dating. However, some aspects are still poorly documented.

In the first place, not enough is known about Neolithic Man and Woman themselves. For the early stages covered by this book we have few skeletal remains outside the Tagus shell-middens, but individual burials occur throughout the Early and Middle Neolithic, which, with the contents of the collective tombs, should provide valuable data when re-examined with a genetic approach. Such studies might provide support for the hypothesis, based on pottery style development and advanced at various points during the book, that in many areas populations were static throughout much of the Neolithic. It may be possible, for instance, to correlate changes in skull shape with changes in diet, rather than to invoke infiltration of new populations. Use of blood grouping techniques may reveal the presence of family or clan groups in separate tombs or areas of tombs, and regional comparisons of populations may be possible using the same means.

For better social and economic information, excavation over much wider areas is necessary. The use of water-sieving can improve our knowledge of the use of domesticated and wild plants, fish and molluscs, and the study of topography, soils, charcoal and pollen will make clearer the type of occupation at each site. Re-working of many older faunal samples is necessary to check to what extent 'wild' species are being managed by human groups, and precise sampling of faunal remains from new excavations will make the proportions of different species being exploited, and the herding and butchering techniques employed, more understandable.

It seems possible that the slow and uneven adoption of farming techniques in West Mediterranean Europe is due in general to the favourable natural resources of the area, in much the same way that aboriginal Californians preferred exploiting natural resources to farming like their neighbours in the American South-West. The varied nature of the terrain meant that numerous types of plant and animal food were available, enabling pre-pottery groups to make a choice of food sources. Farming was adopted to a greater or lesser degree as one more resource, but many generations passed before it ousted the majority of naturally occurring foodstuffs. Jarman has provided an excellent model of this slow but inexorable change in his work on North Italy (Jarman, 1971). By contrast, South-East Italy had a well-established farming economy in the fifth millennium b.c.

Southern France was one of the areas where animal herding probably began before pottery was first used, and was also the home of some of the earliest Neolithic settlers known to us. Two thousand years later, Chasséen economy was firmly based on herding, especially of cattle and sheep, and on domesticated crops, although many other foodstuffs were used to complement the diet in different districts. Farming continued as a basic strategy into the Late Neolithic, probably with more extreme local variations of emphasis on the different domesticated animals and crops.

Economic evidence about the Iberian peninsula is at present very widely scattered in space and time. In the mid-fifth millennium b.c. domesticated crops were being grown in Eastern and Southern Spain. These areas seem to have been isolated from Portugal, where there is no clear evidence for farming until the Late Neolithic. By the third millennium b.c. rich and successful societies with fortified settlements emerge in Portugal and South-East Spain, and it seems unlikely that they were not based on farming.

Our knowledge of the economies of the Mediterranean islanders is also rather sparse, although again it seems inherently likely, for instance, that the Tarxien culture of Malta or the San Michele culture in the fertile North-West of Sardinia, were agriculturally based.

A tentative model for economic strategies in West Mediterranean Europe over the millennia in question might be that from a primarily land-based economy in the Mesolithic there was a shift to a primarily sea-based economy in the sixth and fifth millennia. The economy swung back to land orientation in the fourth millennium. From *circa* 3000 to *circa* 2000 b.c., although subsistence was land-based, much more extensive exchanges of goods and ideas occurred, which must have been based on sea communications.

The model accounts for the phenomena of several broad stylistic regions, separated by geographical barriers, in the Mesolithic, and for the similarities of pottery and other artifact types over coastal zones throughout West Mediterranean Europe during the Early Neolithic.

In the fourth millennium b.c. there is a more inland orientation, so that again cultural differences occur either side of geographical barriers such as the Pyrenees and the Alps. Within topographical boundaries there is substantial similarity of material culture. Finally, in the third millennium, considerable variety in material culture occurs between local areas, reflecting the size and richness of different societies, but there is marked cross-cultural similarity in the form of funerary architecture and trade items.

The area under discussion did not operate in isolation during the Neolithic. Southern Italy and Sicily were probably influenced from the Eastern Mediterranean, Northern Italy and Southern France from the continental areas to the North of them, and Sardinia and Southern Spain possibly from North Africa. Nevertheless, in the model suggested above, West Mediterranean Europe shows considerable general uniformity of development from the final Mesolithic to the beginning of the Bronze Age, and provides a picture of gradual cultural and economic change which can probably be paralleled in other environmentally favoured areas of the world where alternative subsistence strategies are offered freely and not under duress.

An outstanding aspect of West Mediterranean life during the Neolithic is the origin of the ancestor cult in two widely separated areas and its spread over the entire region. It is fitting, within the general context of continuity and evolution that has been sketched out in this book, that collective burial and the ancestor cult continue into the Bronze Age, and that it is necessary to call a halt in the middle of the story.

# Bibliography

Non-standard abbreviations are as follows:
> BMAPM *Bulletin du Musée d'Anthropologie Préhistorique de Monaco*
> BSPF *Bulletin de la Société Préhistorique Française.* Here the reference
is normally to the yearly volume of *Etudes et Travaux,* but where the
monthly *Comptes Rendus* are referred to this is indicated below:
crsm *Comptes Rendus des Séances Mensuelles*

Abelanet, J. and Charles, R. P., 1964, Un site du Néolithique Ancien en Roussillon, La Cova de l'Espérit. *Cahiers Ligures,* 13: pp. 177–206

Admiralty, 1941, *Spain and Portugal,* vol. I, Geographical Handbook Series BR 502. Naval Intelligence Division

Admiralty, 1942a, *France,* vol. I, Geographical Handbook Series BR 503. Naval Intelligence Division

Admiralty, 1942b, *Corsica,* Geographical Handbook Series BR 508. Naval Intelligence Division

Admiralty, 1944, *Italy,* vol. I, Geographical Handbook Series BR 517. Naval Intelligence Division

Alessio, M. and Bella, F., 1969, University of Rome Carbon-14 dates: VII. *Radiocarbon,* 11–2, pp. 482–98

Alessio, M., Bella, F., Bachechi, B. and Cortesi, C., 1966, University of Rome Carbon-14 dates IV. *Radiocarbon,* 8, pp. 401–12

Alessio, M., Bella, F., Cortesi, C. and Graziadei, B., 1964, University of Rome Carbon-14 dates II. *Radiocarbon,* 6, pp. 77–90

Alessio, M., Bella, F., Cortesi, C. and Graziadei, B., 1968, University of Rome Carbon-14 dates VI. *Radiocarbon,* 10, pp. 350–64

Almagro, M., 1962, El poblado de Almizaraque de Herrerías (Almería). *Sixth International Congress of Prehistoric and Protohistoric Sciences* II, pp. 378–9

Almagro, M., 1970, Las fechas C 14 para la prehistoria y la arqueología peninsular. *Trabajos de Prehistoria,* 27, pp. 9–43

Almagro, M. and Arribas, A., 1963, *El poblado y la necrópolis megalítica de Los Millares.* Bibliotheca Praehistorica España III, Madrid

Ammerman, A., 1971a, *Some Aspects of Italian Prehistory 10,000 B.C. to circa 5,500 B.C.,* PhD thesis, University of London p 38 /

Ammerman, A., 1971b, A Computer Analysis of Epipalaeolithic Assemblages in Italy, *in Mathematics in the Archaeological and Historical*

*Sciences* (ed F. R. Hodson, D. G. Kendall and P. Tautu). Edinburgh University Press

Ammerman, A. and Hodson, R., 1972, Constellation Analysis: A Study of Late Palaeolithic Assemblages in Italy. *Riv. Sci. Preist.*, 27, pp. 323–44

Ammerman, A. and Pollnac, R., 1973, A Multivariate Analysis of Late Palaeolithic Assemblages in Italy *in The Explanation of Culture Change* (ed C. Renfrew). Duckworth, London

Anati, E., 1960, La grande roche de Naquane. *Archives de l'Institut de Paléontologie Humaine, Memoire 31.* Masson, Paris

Anati, E., 1963, La datazione dell'arte preistorica camuna. *Studi Camuni* 2, Tipografia Camuna, Breno

Arias-Radi, G., Bigazzi, G. and Bonadonna, F., 1972, Le Tracce di Fissione come possibile metodo per lo studio delle vie di commercio dell'ossidiana. *Origini* 6, pp. 155–70

Arnal, G. B., 1970, Le Néolithique récent dans la stratigraphie de Saint-Etienne-de-Gourgas, *in Les Civilisations Néolithiques du Midi de la France* (ed J. Guilaine) pp. 104–5

Arnal, J., 1963, Les dolmens du Département de l'Hérault. *Préhistoire* 15. Presses Univ. de France, Paris

Arnal, J., Burnez, C., and Larroque-Roussot, J., 1967, Sauvetage de la station fontbuxienne du Gravas, Saint-Mathieu-de-Tréviers (Hérault). *BSPF,* 64, pp. 527–86

Arnal, J. and Hugues, C., 1963, Sur les statues-menhirs du Languedoc-Rouergue (France). *Archivo Prehistoria Levantina,* 10, pp. 23-38

Arnal, J., Hugues, C. and Rodriguez, G., 1966, La statue-menhir de Foumendouyre. *Congrès Préhistorique de France* (Ajaccio) pp. 379–88. Paris

Arnal, J., Latour, J. and Riquet, R., 1953, Les hypogées et stations néolithiques de la région d'Arles-en-Provence. *Etudes Roussillonnaises,* 3, pp. 27–69

Arnal, J., Lorblanchet, M. and Peyrolles, D., 1966, Fouilles dans le gisement de Fontbouisse (Villevieille, Gard). *Ogam,* 18, pp. 189–202

Arnal, J., Prades, H. and Fletcher, D., 1968, *La Ereta del Castellar* (*Villafranca del Cid, Castellón*). Servicio de Investigacion Prehistórica, Valencia. Serie de Trabajos Varios 35

Arnal, J. and Robert, A., 1967, Le Château du Lébous. *Pyrenae,* 3, pp. 17–32

Arnal, J. and Rodriguez, G., 1971, Le gisement saintponien de Dorio, Félines-Minervois (Hérault). *BMAPM,* 17, pp. 171–90

Arribas, A., 1968, Las bases económicas del Neolítico al Bronce *in Estudios de Economía Antigua de la Península Ibérica* (ed M. Tarradell), pp. 33–60

Arribas, A., 1972, Das Neolithikum Andalusiens, *in Die Anfänge des Neolithikums vom Orient bis Nordeuropa* (ed H. Schwabedissen) VII, pp. 108–27. Cologne

Atzeni, E., 1966, L'abri sous roche D' du village préhistorique de

## 158  Bibliography

Filitosa (Sollacaro, Corse). *Congrès Préhistorique de France* (Ajaccio), pp. 169–92. Paris

Audibert, J., 1958, Préhistoire de la Sardaigne, résultats de mission archéologique. *BMAPM,* 5, pp. 189–246

Audibert, J. and Hugues, C., 1956, Céramiques Cardiales du Gard. *Congrès Préhistorique de France* (Angoulême), pp. 190–8

Azzi, C. M., Bigliocca, L. and Piovan, E., 1973, Florence Radiocarbon Dates I. *Radiocarbon,* 15, pp. 479–87

Bagolini, B., 1971a, Considerazioni preliminari sull'industria litica dei livelli neolitici di Romagnano-Trento (Scavi 1969–70). *Preistoria Alpina. Rendiconti,* 7, pp. 107–33. Trento

Bagolini, B., 1971b, Ricerche sulla tipometria litica dei complessi epipaleolitici della Valle dell'Adige. *Preistoria Alpina. Rendiconti,* 7, pp. 243–76. Trento

Bagolini, B. and Barfield, L., 1970, Il neolitico di Chiozza di Scandiaon nell'ambito delle culture padane. *Società di Cultura Preistorica Tridentina-Trento. Rendiconti,* 6, pp. 107–78

Bagolini B., Barfield, L. and Broglio, A., 1973, Notizie preliminari sulle ricerche nell'insediamento neolitico di Fimon – Molino, Casarotto (Vicenza) (1969–72). *Riv. Sci. Preist.,* 27–1, pp. 161–215

Bagolini, B. and de Marinis, R. 1973, Scoperte di arte neolitica al Riparo Gaban (Trento). *Bollettino del Centro Camuno di Studi Preistorici,* 10, pp. 59–78

Bailloud, G., 1969, Fouille d'un habitat néolithique et torréen à Basi (Serra-di-Ferro, Corse). Premiers résultats. *BSPF,* 66, pp. 367–84

Bailloud, G., 1972, Datations C 14 pour le site de Basi (Serra-di-Ferro, Corse). *BSPF,* 69, crsm, 3 pp. 71–2

Bailloud, G., 1973, Les habitations chalcolithiques de Conquette (Saint-Martin-de-Londres, Hérault), *in L'Homme, Hier et Aujourd'hui* (Recueil d'études en hommage à André Leroi-Gourhan), pp. 493–504. Cujas, Paris

Balsan, L. and Costantini G., 1972, La Grotte I des Treilles à Saint-Jean et Saint-Paul (Aveyron). *Gallia Préhistoire,* 15, pp. 229–59

Barfield, L., 1966, Excavations on the Rocca di Rivoli (Verona) 1963 *Memorie del Museo Civico di Storia Naturale, Verona,* 14, pp. 1–100

Barfield, L., 1971, *Northern Italy Before Rome.* Thames & Hudson, London

Barker, G., 1972, The conditions of cultural and economic growth in the Bronze Age of Central Italy. *PPS,* 38, pp. 170–208

Barker, G., 1974a, *Prehistoric Economies and Cultures in Central Italy.* PhD thesis, University of Cambridge

Barker, G., 1974b, Prehistoric territories and economies in Central Italy, *in Palaeoeconomy* (ed E. S. Higgs): 111–75. Cambridge

Barral, L. and Simone, S., 1968, *Préhistoire de la Côte d'Azur Orientale et Musée d'Anthropologie Préhistorique de Monaco.* Monaco

Barrès, E., 1953, Quatre stations préhistoriques des environs de Montpellier. *Rivista di Studi Liguri,* 19, pp. 75–8

Barrière, C., 1965, *Les Civilisations Tardenoisiennes en Europe Occidentale.* Bière, Paris

Barrière, C., 1965a, Flore et Faune de Rouffignac (Dordogne). *Annales de la Faculté des Lettres et Sciences Humaines de Toulouse,* 1–5, pp. 7–11

Barrière, C., 1965b, Le gisement de la grotte de Rouffignac (Dordogne). *Atti del 6° Congresso Internazionale delle Scienze Preistoriche e Protostoriche,* 2, pp. 157–60. Rome

Barrière, C., 1974, Rouffignac. Fasc. 1, *Mémoire de l'Institut d'Art Préhistorique* II. Publications de L'Institut d'Art Préhistorique de l'Université de Toulouse. Le Mirail

Bernabò Brea, L., 1946, *Gli scavi nella caverna delle Arene Candide.* Parte I, Gli strati con ceramiche. Bordighera

Bernabò Brea, L., 1956, *Gli scavi nella caverna delle Arene Candide.* Parte I, Gli strati con ceramiche vol. 2, Bordighera

Bernabò Brea, L., 1957, *Sicily before the Greeks.* Thames & Hudson, London

Bernabò Brea, L. and Cavalier, M., 1960, *Meligunìs-Lipára* vol. I. Flaccovio, Palermo

Binford, L., 1962, Archaeology as Anthropology. *American Antiquity,* 28, pp. 217–25

Bonuccelli, G. and Faedo, L., 1968, Il villaggio a ceramica impressa di Capo d'Acqua. *Atti della Società Toscana di Scienze Naturali,* 75, pp. 87–101

Bordes, F., 1950, Principes d'une méthode d'étude des techniques et de la typologie du Paléolithique Ancien et Moyen. *L'Anthropologie,* 54, pp. 19–34

Bordreuil, M., 1966, Recherches sur les perles à ailettes. *Congrès Préhistorique de France* (Ajaccio) pp. 169–92. Paris

Bordreuil, M., 1974, Les mines de silex néolithiques dans le Gard *BSPF,* 71, crsm, 2, p. 34

Bosch-Gimpera, P., 1969, La cultura de Almería. *Pyrenae,* 5, pp. 47–93

Bousquet, N., Gourdiole, R. and Guiraud, R., 1966, La grotte de Labeil près de Laroux (Hérault). *Cahiers Ligures,* 15, pp. 79–166

Bray, W., 1963, The Ozieri Culture of Sardinia. *Riv. Sci. Preist.,* 18, pp. 155–208

Broglio, A., 1971, Risultati preliminari delle ricerche sui complessi epipaleolitici della Valle dell'Adige. *Preistoria Alpina. Rendiconti,* 7, pp. 135–241

Broglio, A., 1972, Cronologia delle culture del Paleolitico superiore, dell'Epipaleolitico e del Neolitico della Valle Padana. *Bollettino del Centro Camuno di Studi Preistorici,* 8, pp. 47–79

Broglio, A., 1973, La preistoria della Valle Padana dalla fine del

Paleolitico agli inizi del Neolitico: cronologia, aspetti culturali e trasformazioni economiche. *Riv. Sci. Preist.,* 27, pp. 133–60

Bryson, R. A., Lamb, H. H. and Donley, D. L., 1974, Drought and the decline of Mycenae. *Antiquity,* 48, pp. 46–50

Calvet, A., 1969, *Les Abris sous roche de Saint-Mitre à Reillanne* (*Basses-Alpes*). Rico, Manosque

Cann, J. R. and Renfrew, C., 1964, The characterization of obsidian and its application to the Mediterranean region. *PPS,* 30, pp. 111–33

Cannarella, D. and Cremonesi, G., 1967, Gli scavi nella Grotta Azzurra di Samatorza nel Carso Triestino. *Riv. Sci. Preist.,* 22, pp. 281–330

Cardini, L., 1946, Gli strati mesolitici e paleolitici della Caverna delle Arene Candide. *Rivista di Studi Liguri,* 12, pp. 29–37

Cardini, L., 1970, Praia a Mare: relazione degli scavi 1957–1970. *Boll. Paletnol. Ital.* ns, 21, pp. 31–59

Carta, E., 1966–7, Documenti del Neolitico Antico nella Grotta 'Rifugio' di Oliena (Nuoro). *Studi Sardi,* 20, pp. 48–67

Castelfranco, P., 1916, *Cimeli del Museo Ponti nell'Isola Virginia* (*Lago di Varese*). Milan

Cazzella, A., 1972, Considerazioni su alcuni aspetti eneolitici dell' Italia meridionale e della Sicilia. *Origini,* 6, pp. 171–299

Ceruti, M., 1967, Domus de jana in località Monumentos (Benetutti, Sassari). *Boll. Paletnol. Ital.,* 18, pp. 69–136

Cianfarani, V., Cremonesi, G. and Radmilli, A. M., 1962, *Trecentomila Anni di Vita in Abruzzo.* Soprintendenza alle Antichità degli Abruzzi e del Molise. Chieti

Clark, J. G. D., 1970, *Aspects of Archaeology.* University of California Press

Clark, R. M. and Renfrew, A. C., 1972, A statistical approach to the calibration of floating tree-ring chronologies using radiocarbon dates. *Archaeometry,* 14, pp. 5–19

Clarke, D., 1968, *Analytical Archaeology.* Methuen, London

Clottes, J., 1969, *Le Lot Préhistorique.* Société des Etudes Littéraires, Scientifiques et Artistiques du Lot. Bulletin 90. Delsaud, Cahors

Clottes, J., 1970, Rapport général sur le mégalithisme méridional *in Les Civilisations Néolithiques du Midi de la France* (ed J. Guilaine), pp. 65–8

Clottes, J. and Lorblanchet, M., 1972, La grotte du Noyer (Esclauzels, Lot). *Congrès Préhistorique de France* (Auvergne 1969), pp. 145–64

Colomines i Roca, J., 1925, Prehistoria de Montserrat. *Analecta Monteserratensia,* 6, pp. 225–352

Constans, L. A., 1921, *Arles Antique.* Boccard, Paris

Contu, E., 1964, *La tomba dei vasi tetrapodi in località Santu Pedru* (*Alghero–Sassari*). Monumenti Antichi, 47. Accademia Nazionale dei Lincei, Rome

Contu, E., 1965, Nuovi petroglifi schematici della Sardegna. *Boll. Palet. Ital.,* 16, pp. 69–122

Contu, E., 1970, Notizario. *Riv. Sci. Preist.*, 25, pp. 432–7

Contu, E., 1971, Notizario. *Riv. Sci. Preist.*, 26, pp. 497–9

Costantini, G., 1967, Chalcolithique et céramique à triangles hachurés des Grands Causses. *BSPF*, 64, crsm, 3, pp. 743–54

Costantini, G., 1970, L'évolution du Chasséen caussenard; l'évolution du Chalcolithique caussenard, *in Les Civilisations Néolithiques du Midi de la France* (ed J. Guilaine), pp. 31–3, 95–8

Courtin, J., 1959, La Grotte de l'Eglise à Baudinard (Var). *Cahiers Ligures*, 8, pp. 211–13

Courtin, J., 1961a, La sépulture chalcolithique du Perpétairi à Mollans (Drôme). *Gallia Préhistoire*, 4, pp. 192–205

Courtin, J., 1961b, La préhistoire récente de la vallée du Verdon. *Cahiers Ligures*, 10, pp. 183–91

Courtin, J., 1962, Le Chalcolithique au Sud du Mont Ventoux. *Bulletin de la Société d'Etude des Sciences Naturelles de Vaucluse* (1957–62), pp. 3–14

Courtin, J., 1967a, La Grotte de l'Eglise à Baudinard (Var). *Gallia Préhistoire*, 10, pp. 282–300

Courtin, J., 1967b, Le problème de l'obsidienne dans le Néolithique du Midi de la France. *Rivista di Studi Liguri*, 33, pp. 93–109

Courtin, J., 1968, Recherches sur le Néolithique provençal. *Cahiers Ligures*, 17, pp. 220–9

Courtin, J., 1970, Le Chasséen méridional *in Les Civilisations Néolithiques du Midi de la France* (ed J. Guilaine), pp. 27–31

Courtin, J., 1972a, Quelques nouvelles datations du Néolithique provençal. *BSPF*, 69, crsm, 4, pp. 118–20

Courtin, J., 1972b, Vase néolithique ancien à anses superposées découvert à Ensuès près de Marseille (Bouches-du-Rhône). *BSPF*, 69, pp. 533–7

Courtin, J., 1973, Datation C 14 du Mésolithique de la Baume Fontbrégoua, à Salernes (Var). *BSPF*, 70, crsm, 4, pp. 99–100

Courtin, J., 1974, *Le Néolithique de la Provence*. Mémoires de la Société Préhistorique Française n. 11. Klincksieck, Paris

Courtin, J., 1974, [*in press*] Le Néolithique Ancien de la Provence. *Actes du Colloque sur l'Epipaléolithique, Aix 1972*

Courtin, J. and Froget, C., 1970, La station néolithique de l'Ile Riou. *BMAPM*, 15, pp. 147–57

Courtin, J., Gagnière, S., Granier, J., Ledoux, J. C. and Onoratini, G., 1970–2, La Grotte du Cap Ragnon, commune du Rove (Bouches-du-Rhône). *Bulletin de la Société d'Etude des Sciences Naturelles de Vaucluse 1970–2*, pp. 113–70

Courtin, J. and Masse, J. P., 1967, Découverte d'une nouvelle maillet à rainure en Basse-Provence. *BSPF*, 64, crsm, 2, pp. LVIII–LXIII

Courtin, J. and Pélouard, S., 1971, Un habitat chasséen en Haute Provence: la 'Grotte C' de Baudinard (Var). *BSPF*, 68, pp. 540–66

L

Cremonesi, G., 1965, Il villaggio di Ripoli alla luce dei recenti scavi. *Riv. Sci. Preist.*, 20, pp. 85–155

Cremonesi, G., 1966, Il villaggio Leopardi presso Penne in Abruzzo *Boll. Paletnol. Ital.*, ns, 17, pp. 27–49

Cremonesi, G., 1968a, Contributo alla conoscenza della preistoria del Fucino: La Grotta di Ortucchio e la Grotta la Punta. *Riv. Sci. Preist.*, 23, pp. 145–204

Cremonesi, G., 1968b, La Grotta dell'Orso di Sarteano – i livelli dell'età dei metalli. *Origini*, 2, pp. 247–331

Damon, P., Long, A. and Wallace, E., 1973, Dendrochronologic Calibration of the Carbon-14 time scale. *Proceedings 8th International Conference on Radio Carbon Dating*. Lower Hutt City, New Zealand, pp. A28–33

Daniel, G., 1960, *The prehistoric chamber tombs of France: a geographical, morphological and chronological survey*. Thames & Hudson, London

Davidson, I., 1972, The animal economy of La Cueva del Volcan del Faro, Spain. *Trans. Cave Research Group of Great Britain*, 14, pp. 23–31

Delibrias, G., Guillier, M. T. and Labeyrie, J., 1974, Gif Radiocarbon Measurements VIII. *Radiocarbon*, 16–1, pp. 15–94

Dixon, J. E., Cann, J. R. and Renfrew, C., 1968, Obsidian and the Origins of Trade. *Sci. Amer.*, 218, 3, pp. 38–46

Ducos, P., 1958, Le gisement de Châteauneuf-les-Martigues (Bouches-du-Rhône); les mammifères et les problèmes de la domestication. *BMAPM*, 5, pp. 119–33

Durante Pasa, M. V. and Pasa, A., 1956, Analisi polliniche e microstratigrafiche nella torbiera della Lagozza. *Memorie del Museo Civico di Storia Naturale di Verona*, 5, pp. 217 ff.

Emiliani, C., Cardini, L., Mayeda, T., MacBurney, C. and Tongiorgi, E., 1964, Palaeotemperature analysis of fossil shells of marine mollusks (food refuse) from the Arene Candide cave, Italy, and the Haua Fteah cave, Cyrenaica. *Isotopic and Cosmic Chemistry* (ed H. Craig), pp. 133–56

Escalon de Fonton, M., 1956, Préhistoire de la Basse Provence. *Préhistoire*, 12

Escalon de Fonton M., 1963, Informations archéologiques. Circonscription des Antiquités Préhistoriques Montpellier. *Gallia Préhistoire*, 6, pp. 235–73

Escalon de Fonton, M., 1966a, Informations archéologiques. Circonscription des Antiquités Préhistoriques Languedoc-Roussillon. *Gallia Préhistoire*, 9, pp. 545–83

Escalon de Fonton, M., 1966b, Origine et développement des civilisations néolithiques méditerranéennes en Europe occidentale. *Palaeohistoria*, 12, pp. 209–48

Escalon de Fonton, M., 1967, Les séquences sédimento-climatiques du Midi méditerranéen du Würm à l'Holocène. *BMAPM*, 14, pp. 125–85

Escalon de Fonton, M., 1968a, L'abri de St Privat et le climat au Subboréal dans le Midi méditerranéen. *BSPF*, 65, pp. 391–8

Escalon de Fonton, M., 1968b, Informations archéologiques. Circonscription des Antiquités Préhistoriques Languedoc-Roussillon. *Gallia Préhistoire*, 11, pp. 463–92

Escalon de Fonton, M., 1970a, Recherches sur la Préhistoire dans le Midi de la France. *Cahiers Ligures*, 19, pp. 97–115

Escalon de Fonton, M., 1970b, Informations archéologiques. Circonscription des Antiquités Préhistoriques Languedoc–Roussillon. *Gallia Préhistoire*, 13, pp. 513–49

Escalon de Fonton, M., 1971, Les Premiers Hommes, *in Documents de l'Histoire de Provence* (ed E. Privat), pp. 7–22. Toulouse

Evans, J. D., 1959, *Malta*. Thames and Hudson, London

Evans, J. D., 1971, *Prehistoric Antiquities of the Maltese Islands: a survey*. Athlone, London

Evett, D. and Renfrew, J. M., 1971, D'agricoltura neolitica italiana: una nota sui cereali. *Riv. Sci. Preist.*, 26, pp. 403–9  *p g 4o q*

Evin, J., Marien, G. and Pachiaudi, C., 1973, Lyon Natural Radiocarbon Measurements IV. *Radiocarbon*, 15–3, pp. 514–33

Fédération Archéologique Hérault (FAH), 1973, *Fiche d'Information No. 2. Bibliographie du Cardial et du Néolithique Ancien*

Ferrara, G., Reinharz, M. and Tongiorgi, E., 1959, Carbon-14 Dating in Pisa. *Radiocarbon Supplement*, 1, pp. 103–10

Fortea, J., 1971, *La Cueva de la Cocina*. Servicio de Investigacion Prehistorica, Valencia. Serie de Trabajos Varios 40

Fournier, E. and Repelin, J., 1901, *Recherches sur le Préhistorique de la Basse-Provence*. Bourlatier, Marseille

Fusco, V. and Guerreschi, G., 1966, Primi risultati della revisione del materiale degli scavi all'Isolino di Varese. *Atti della X^a Riunione Scientifica dell'Istituto Italiano di Preistoria e Protostoria*, pp. 147–54

Gagnière, S., 1961, Informations archéologiques. Circonscription des Antiquités Préhistoriques Aix-en-Provence. *Gallia Préhistoire*, 4, pp. 377–86

Gagnière, S., 1963, Informations archéologiques. Circonscription des Antiquités Préhistoriques Aix-en-Provence. *Gallia Préhistoire*, 6, pp. 337–49

Gagnière, S., 1966, Informations archéologiques. Circonscription des Antiquités Préhistoriques Provence-Cote d'Azur-Corse. *Gallia Préhistoire*, 9, pp. 585–622

Gagnière, S., 1968, Informations archéologiques. Circonscription des Antiquités Préhistoriques Provence-Cote d'Azur-Corse. *Gallia Préhistoire*, 11, pp. 493–528

Gagnière, S., 1970, Informations archéologiques. Circonscription des Antiquités Préhistoriques Provence-Cote d'Azur-Corse. *Gallia Préhistoire*, 13, pp. 551–83

Gagnière, S., 1972, Informations archéologiques. Circonscription des Antiquités Préhistoriques Provence-Côte d'Azur-Corse. *Gallia Préhistoire,* 15, pp. 537–69

Gagnière, S. and Granier, J., 1963, Les stèles anthropomorphes du Musée Calvet d'Avignon. *Gallia Préhistoire,* 6, pp. 31–62

Gagnière, S. and Granier, J., 1967, Nouvelles stèles anthropomorphes chalcolithiques de la vallée de la Durance. *BSPF,* 64, pp. 699–706

Gagnière, S. and Granier, J., [not dated] Nouvelles découvertes archéologiques au Quartier de la Balance à Avignon, *in Guide Illustré d'Avignon.* Marcelle, Avignon

Gagnière, S., Lanfranchi, F., de Miskovsky, J. C., Prost, M., Renault-Miskovsky, J. and Weiss, M. C., 1969, L'abri d'Araguina-Sennola à Bonifacio (Corse) *BSPF,* 66, pp. 385–418    *P9 3 88*

Galan, A., 1967, La station néolithique de la Perte du Cros à Saillac (Lot). *Gallia Préhistoire,* 10, pp. 1–73

Galy, G., 1971, La transition Mésolithique-Néolithique en France, *in Die Anfänge des Neolithikums vom Orient bis Nordeuropa* (ed H. Schwabedissen), Vol. 6, pp. 79–99

Gambassini, P. and Palma di Cesnola, A., 1967, Resti di villaggi neolitici a ceramiche impresse a Trinitapoli (Foggia). *Riv. Sci. Preist.,* 22, pp. 331–48

Gill, E. D., 1971, The Paris Symposium on World Sealevels of the past 11,000 years. *Quaternaria,* 14, pp. 1–6

Glassow, M., 1972, Changes in the Adaptation of Southwestern Basketmakers, *in Contemporary Archaeology* (ed M. Leone), pp. 289–302

Grifoni, R. and Radmilli, A. M., 1964, La Grotta Maritza e il Fucino primo dell'età romana. *Riv. Sci. Preist.,* 19, pp. 53–127

Grosjean, R., 1966, *La Corse avant l'Histoire.* Klincksieck, Paris

Grosjean, R., 1971, La Préhistoire, *in Histoire de la Corse* (ed P. Arrighi), pp. 11–33. Privat, Toulouse

Groupe d'Etude de L'Epipaléolithique-Mésolithique (GEEM), 1969, Epipaléolithique-Mésolithique. Les microlithes géometriques. *BSPF,* 66, pp. 355–66

Groupe d'Etude de l'Epipaléolithique-Mésolithique (GEEM), 1972, Epi-paléolithique-Mésolithique. Les armatures non géometriques. *BSPF,* 69, pp. 364–75

Guerreschi, G., 1967, *La Lagozza di Besnate e il Neolitico Superiore Padano.* Noseda, Como

Guido, M., 1963, *Sardinia.* Thames and Hudson, London

Guilaine, J., 1966, Datation C 14 d'un gisement néolithique du Sud de la France. *Archivo de Prehistoria Levantina,* 11, pp. 75–80

Guilaine, J., 1967, *La Civilisation du Vase Campaniforme dans les Pyrénées Françaises.* Gabelle, Carcassonne

Guilaine, J., 1968, Recherches de Préhistoire récente en Languedoc occidental. Campagne de fouilles 1967. *Cahiers Ligures,* 17, pp. 236–42

Guilaine, J. (ed), 1970a, *Les civilisations néolithiques du Midi de la* France. Carcassonne: Laboratoire de Préhistoire et de Palethnologie

Guilaine, J., 1970b, Recherches de Préhistoire récente en Languedoc occidental et Roussillon. *Cahiers Ligures,* 19, pp. 149–74

Guilaine, J., 1970c, Les fouilles de la Grotte de Gazel (Sallèles-Cabardès, Aude). *Bulletin de la Société d'Etudes Scientifiques de l'Aude,* 70, pp. 61–73 *pg 62-4*

Guilaine, J., 1971a, La néolithisation du bassin de l'Aude et des Pyrénées méditerranéennes françaises, *in Die Anfänge des Neolithikums vom Orient pg 118 bis Nordeuropa* (ed H. Schwabedissen), 6, pp. 100–21

Guilaine, J., 1971b, Recherches de Préhistoire récente en Languedoc occidental. Campagne de Fouilles 1971. *Cahiers Ligures,* 20, pp. 183–95

Guilaine, J., 1974, *La Balma de Montbolo, et le Néolithique de l'Occident Méditerranéen.* Institut Pyrénéen d'Etudes Anthropologiques

Guilaine, J. and Calvet, A., 1970, Nouveaux points de chronologie absolue pour le Néolithique ancien de la Meditérranée occidentale. *L'Anthropologie,* 73, pp. 85–92

Guilaine, J. and da Veiga, O., 1970, Le Néolithique ancien au Portugal. *BSPF,* 67, pp. 304–22

Guilaine, J. and Muñoz, A. M., 1964, La civilisation catalane des 'sepulcros de fosa' et les sépultures néolithiques du Sud de la France. *Rivista di Studi Liguri,* 30, pp. 5–30

Guilaine, J. and Vaquer, J., 1973, Le site chasséen d'Auriac, commune de Carcassonne (Aude). *BSPF,* 70, pp. 367–84

Gumerman, G., 1973, The reconciliation of theory and method in archaeology, *in Research and Theory in Current Archaeology* (ed C. L. Redman), pp. 287–99

Hallam, B. and Warren, S., 1973, Neutron Activation Analysis of West Mediterranean Obsidian (paper to Oxford Conference on Archaeomagnetism and Archaeological Prospection)

Hallam, B., Warren, S. and Renfrew, C., [In preparation] Obsidian in the Western Mediterranean: Characterisation by Neutron Activation Analysis and Optical Emission Spectroscopy

Harrison, R., 1974, Origins of the Bell Beaker Cultures. *Antiquity,* 48, pp. 99–109

Hassko, B., Guillet, B., Jaegy, R. and Coppens, R., 1974, Nancy Natural Radiocarbon Measurements III. *Radiocarbon,* 16–1, pp. 118–30

Higgs, E. S. (ed), 1972, *Papers in Economic Prehistory.* Cambridge University Press

Hopf, M., 1964, Triticum monococcum L. y Triticum dicoccum Schübl, en el neolitico antiguo español. *Archivo de Prehistoria Levantina,* 11, pp. 53–73

Hopf, M., 1971, Vorgeschichtliche Pfanzenreste aus Ostspanien. *Madrider Mitteilungen,* 12, pp. 101–14

Hopf, M. and Pellicer, M., 1970, Neolitische Getreidefunde in der Höhle von Nerja (prov. Malaga). *Madrider Mitteilungen,* 11, pp. 18–34

Hugues, C. and Jeantet, J., 1967, Les statues-menhirs du Musée d'Histoire Naturelle de Nîmes. *Rivista di Studi Liguri,* 33, pp. 131–49

Jarman, M., 1971, Culture and economy in the North Italian Neolithic. *Word Archaeology,* 2, pp. 255–65

Jarman, M., 1972, European deer economies and the advent of the Neolithic, *in Papers in Economic Prehistory* (ed E. S. Higgs), pp. 125–47

Jarman, M. and Webley, D., 1974, Settlement and Land Use in Capitanata, Italy, *in Palaeoeconomy* (ed E. S. Higgs), Cambridge University Press

Jorda Cerdá, F., 1959, Los enterramientos de la Cueva de la Torre del Mal Paso. *Archivo de Prehistoria Levantina,* 7, pp. 55–92

Jorda Cerdá, F., 1966, Notas para una revisíon de la cronología del arte rupestre Levantino. *Zephyrus,* 17, pp. 47–76

Kopper, J. and Waldren, W., 1967–8, Balearic Prehistory. A New Perspective. *Archaeology,* pp. 20–1, 108–115

Lanfranchi, F. de, 1972, L'abri sous roche no. 1 de la station de Curacchiaghiu (Lévie, Corse). *BSPF,* 69, crsm, 3, pp. 70–1

Lanfranchi, F. de, 1973, Le peuplement des hauts bassins du Rizzanese et de l'Ortolo des Origines à l'arrivée des Romains (mimeographed article), pp. 213–56

Lanfranchi, F. de and Weiss, M. C., 1972, Le Néolithique ancien de l'abri d'Araguina-Sennola (Bonifacio, Corse). *BSPF,* 69, pp. 376–88

Lanfranchi, F. de and Weiss, M. C., 1973, *La Civilisation des Corses. Les Origines.* Cyrnos et Méditerranée, Ajaccio

Laplace, G., 1964, Essai de typologie systématique. *Ann. Univ. Ferrara,* ns sec. 15, suppl. 2 to vol. 1

Laplace, G., 1968, Recherches de typologie analytique. *Origini,* 2, pp. 7–64

Larroque-Roussot, J., 1973, Les microlithes et la civilisation d'Artenac en Aquitaine. *BSPF,* 70, crsm, 7, pp. 211–18

Leale Anfassi, M., 1958–61, Revisione dei materiali fittili e faunistici provenienti dagli scavi nella Grotta del Pertusello (Val Pennevaira-Albenga). *Quaternaria* 5, pp. 318–20. Terza Campagna di scavi sistematici all'Arma dello Stefanin (Val Pennavaira-Albenga). *Quaternaria,* 5, pp. 347–8, 357

Leale Anfassi, M., 1972, Il giacimento dell'Arma dello Stefanin (Val Pennavaira-Albenga). *Riv. Sci. Preist.,* 27, pp. 249–321

Leale Anfassi, M., 1962, La scoperta dell'Arma di Nasino. *Rivista Ingauna e Intemelia* ns, 17, pp. 53–5

Leisner, G. and Leisner, V., 1943, *Die Megalithgräber der iberischen Halbinsel, Der Süden.* Römisch-Germanische Forschungen, Band 17. de Gruyter, Berlin

Leisner, G. and Leisner, V., 1956–65, *Die Megalithgräber der Iberischen Halbinsel. Der Westen.* Lieferungen 1–3. Deutsches Archäologisches Institut, Abteilung Madrid. Madrider Forschungen Band I. de Gruyter, Berlin

Leisner, V. 1967, Die verschiedenen Phasen des Neolithikums in Portugal. *Palaeohistoria,* 12, pp. 366–72

Leone, M., 1968, Neolithic Economic Autonomy and Social Distance. *Science,* 162, pp. 1150–1

Leone, M. (ed), 1972, *Contemporary Archaeology.* Southern Illinois University Press

Lilliu, G., 1959, Ricerche sull'Arcipelago de La Maddalena. *Memorie della Società Geografica Italiana,* 25, pp. 5–39

Lilliu, G., 1972, *La Civiltà dei Sardi dal neolitico all'età dei Nuraghi.* E.R.I. (2nd edition), Turin

Lollini, D., 1959a, Notiziario. *Riv. Sci. Preist.,* 14, p. 320

Lollini, D., 1965, Il neolitico nelle Marche alla luce delle recenti scoperte. *Atti 6° Congresso Internazionale delle Scienze Preistoriche e Protostoriche,* 2, pp. 309–15. Rome

Lorblanchet, M., 1965, Contribution à l'étude du peuplement des Grands Causses. *BSPF,* 62, pp. 667–712

Lorblanchet, M., 1970, Le Rodézien, in *Les Civilisations Néolithiques du Midi de la France* (ed J. Guilaine), pp. 98–103

Loria, R., 1971, Figurette schematiche femminili nella ceramica eneolitica della Sardegna. *Riv. Sci. Preist.,* 26, pp. 179–202

Louis, M., 1948, *Préhistoire du Languedoc Méditerranéen et du Roussillon.* Montpellier

Majurel, R. and Pradès, H., 1967, La station de La Condamine (Saint-Aunès, Hérault). *Gallia Préhistoire,* 10, pp. 225–36

Malavolti, F., 1953, *Appunti per una cronologia relativa del neo-eneolitico emiliano.* Centro Emiliano di Studi Preistorici, Modena.

Malenfant, M., Couteaux, M. and Cauvin, J., 1970, Le gisement chasséen de Francin (Savoie). *Gallia Préhistoire,* 13, pp. 25–52

Maluquer de Motes, J., 1972, *Proceso Histórico Económico de la Primitiva Población Peninsular.* Instituto de Arqueología y Prehistoria, Universidad de Barcelona. Publicaciones Eventuales 20

Manfredini, A., 1969, Notiziario. *Riv. Sci. Preist.,* 24, pp. 374–5

Manfredini, A., 1970, Nuove ricerche a Chiozza di Scandiano. *Origini,* 4, pp. 145–59

Manfredini, A., 1972, Il villaggio trincerato di Monte Aquilone nel quadro del neolitico dell'Italia meridionale. *Origini,* 6, pp. 29–154

Martin, L., Nourrit, A., Durand-Tullou, A. and Arnal, G. B., 1964, Les Grottes-Citernes des Causses. *Gallia Préhistoire,* 7, pp. 107–77

Matson, F. (ed), 1965, *Ceramics and Man.* Viking Fund Publications in Anthropology 41

Maury, J., 1967a, *Les étapes de peuplement sur les Grands Causses des origines à l'époque gallo-romaine.* Maury, Millau

Maury, J., 1967b, A propos de quelques datations par le radio-carbone des gisements des Grands Causses. *BSPF,* 64, pp. LXX–LXXI

Maury, J., 1969, *L'Aveyron dans la Préhistoire.* Maury, Millau

Méroc, L., 1959, Informations archéologiques. Circonscription des Antiquités Préhistoriques Midi-Pyrénées. *Gallia Préhistoire,* 2, pp. 133–53

Méroc, L., 1967, Informations archéologiques. Circonscription des Antiquités Préhistoriques Midi-Pyrénées. *Gallia Préhistoire,* 10, pp. 389–411

Méroc, L., 1969, Informations archéologiques. Circonscription des Antiquités Préhistoriques Midi-Pyrénées. *Gallia Préhistoire,* 12, pp. 485–503

Méroc, L. and Simonnet, G., 1969, Le village néolithique Chasséen de Saint-Michel-du-Touch, commune de Toulouse (Haute-Garonne). *Bulletin de la Société Méridionale de Spéléologie et de Préhistoire,* pp. 14–15; 27–37

Méroc, L. and Simonnet, G., 1970, Le Chasséen de la haute et de la moyenne vallée de la Garonne, *in Les Civilisations Néolithiques du Midi de la France* (ed J. Guilaine)

Michael, H. and Ralph, E., 1972, Discussion of Radiocarbon Dates obtained from precisely dated Sequoia and Bristle-cone pine samples, *in Proceedings 8th International Conference on Radiocarbon Dating,* Lower Hutt City, New Zealand, pp. A11–27

Montjardin, R., 1962, Le peuplement préhistorique d'un plateau de la Basse Ardèche: Chauzon. *Cahiers Rhodaniens,* 9, pp. 4–52

Montjardin, R., 1965, Le peuplement préhistorique de Chauzon (Suite). *Cahiers Rhodaniens,* 12, pp. 13–33

Montjardin, R., 1966, Le gisement néolithique d'Escanin aux Baux de la Provence (Bouches-du-Rhône). *Cahiers Rhodaniens,* 13, pp. 5–99

Montjardin, R., 1972–3, Soleils Préhistoriques. *Bulletin de la Société d'Etudes Scientifiques de Sète,* 4, pp. 1–18

Muñoz, A. M., 1965, *La Cultura Neolítica Catalana de los Sepulcros de Fosa.* Barcelona

Muñoz, A. M., 1971, Dos nuevas fechas de C-14 para sepulcros de fosa. *Pyrenae,* 7, pp. 157

Murray, J., 1970, *The first European agriculture.* Edinburgh University Press

Niederlender, A., Lacam, R. and Arnal, J., 1966, *Le Gisement Néolithique de Roucadour* (3rd Supplement to *Gallia Préhistoire*). Paris

Nourrit, A. and Arnal, G. B., 1968, Préhistoire de la région de Ganges. *Cahiers Ligures,* 17, pp. 29–81

Paccard, M., 1954, La grotte d'Unang (Gorges de la Nesque, Mallemort, Vaucluse). *Cahiers Ligures,* 3, pp. 3–25

Paccard, M., 1963, Le gisement préhistorique de Roquefure. *Cahiers Rhodaniens,* 10, pp. 3–36

Paccard, M., 1971, Le Camp Mésolithique de Gramari à Méthamis (Vaucluse). *Gallia Préhistoire,* pp. 14–1; 47–137

Pellicer, M., 1963, Estratigrafía prehistórica de la cueva de Nerja. *Excavaciones Arqueológicas en España,* 16

Pellicer, M., 1964, El neolítico y el bronce de la Cueva de la Cariguela del Piñar. *Trabajos de Prehistoria,* 15. Madrid

Pellicer, M., 1967, Las civilizaciones neolíticas hispanas, *in Las Raíces de España,* Madrid: Instituto Español de Antropología Aplicada, pp. 27–46

Pericot Garcia, L., 1945, La cueva de la Cocina (Dos Aguas). *Archivo de Prehistoria Levantina,* 2, pp. 39–71. Valencia

Pericot Garcia, L., 1972, *The Balearics.* Thames and Hudson, London

Perini, R., 1971, I depositi preistorici di Romagnano-Loc (Trento). *Preistoria Alpina. Rendiconti,* 7, pp. 7–106

Peroni, R., 1962–3, La Romita di Asciano (Pisa). *Boll. Paletnol. Ital.,* pp. 71–2; 251–442

Peroni, R., 1967, *Archeologia della Puglia Preistorica.* De Luca, Rome

Phillips, P., 1971a, *An analysis of the Southern French Chassey culture and its relationship to the Cortaillod and Lagozza cultures.* PhD thesis, University of London

Phillips, P., 1971b, Attribute analysis and social structure of Chassey–Cortaillod–Lagozza populations. *Man,* 6, pp. 341–52

Phillips, P., 1972, Population, economy and society in the Chassey–Cortaillod–Lagozza cultures. *World Archaeology,* 4, pp. 41–56

Phillips, P., 1973, Les caractères régionaux du Chasséen du Midi. *BSPF,* 69, pp. 538–53

Poulain-Josien, T., 1957a, Fonds de cabane chalcolithiques de la Bergerie Neuve à Lauret (Hérault). Etude de la faune. Le gisement chalcolithique d'Anis 2-Hortus à Valflaunès (Hérault). Etude de la faune. *BSPF,* 53, 95–101

Poulain-Josien, T., 1957b, Etude de la faune des stations chalcolithiques de Gimel et de la Paillade, commune de Grabels (Hérault). *BSPF,* 53, pp. 758–62

Poulain-Josien, T., 1965, Gisement de Beaussement: Etude de la Faune. *Cahiers Rhodaniens,* 12, pp. 33–40

Prades, H. and Groupe Archéologique Painlevé, Montpellier 1967, La colonisation antique des rivages lagunaires du Languedoc. *Rivista di Studi Liguri,* 33, pp. 110–30

Puxeddu, C., 1955–7, Giacimenti di ossidiana del Monte Arci in Sardegna e sua irradiazione. *Studi Sardi,* 14–15; 10–66

Radmilli, A. M., 1962, *Piccola Guida della Preistoria Italiana.* Florence

Radmilli, A. M., 1972, Die Neolithisierung Italiens, *in Die Anfänge des Neolithikums vom Orient bis Nordeuropa* (ed H. Schwabedissen), 7, pp. 128–65. Cologne

Ralph, E., Michael, H. and Han, M., 1973, Radiocarbon Dates and Reality. *Masca Newsletter,* 9–1; 1–20

Redman, C. L., (ed) 1973, *Research and Theory in Current Archaeology.* Wiley-Interscience, New York

Renault-Miskovsky, J., 1970, Analyse pollinique des sédiments néolithiques extraits du gisement de La Couronne. *Cahiers Ligures,* 19, pp. 116–18

Renault-Miskovsky, J., 1971, Analyse pollinique des sédiments post-glaciaires de l'abri de Châteauneuf-les-Martigues. *Bulletin de l'Association française pour l'étude du Quaternaire,* 1971–1, pp. 33–46

Renfrew, C., 1967, Colonialism and Megalithismus. *Antiquity,* 41, pp. 276–88

Renfrew, C., 1973, *Before Civilisation: the radiocarbon revolution and prehistoric Europe.* Cape, London

Ribeiro, L. and Sangmeister, E., 1967, Der neolitische Fundplatz von Possanco bei Comporta (Portugal). *Madrider Mitteilungen,* 8, pp. 31–46

Ripoll, E. and Llongueras, M., 1963, *La cultura neolítica de los sepulcros de fosa en Cataluña.* Instituto de Prehistoria y Arqueología, Barcelona. Monografías 21

Ripoll, E. and Llongueras, M., 1967, Notas sobre sepulcros de fosa catalanes *Ampurias,* 29, pp. 240–57

Roche, J., 1960, *Le gisement mésolithique de Moita do Sebastião* Instituto de Alta Cultura, Lisbon

Roche, J., 1965, Observations sur la stratigraphie et la chronologie des amas coquilliers de Muge (Portugal). *BSPF,* 62, pp. 130–8 and LI

Roche, J., 1972, Les amas coquilliers (concheiros) mésolithiques de Muge (Portugal), *in Die Anfänge des Neolithikums vom Orient bis Nord-europa* (ed H. Schwabedissen), 7, pp. 72–107

Rodriguez, G., 1968, Le Néolithique dans le Saintponais (Hérault) *BSPF,* 65, crsm, 3, pp. 699–748

Rodriguez, G., 1970, Grotte de Camprafaud (Hérault). Datations au C-14. *BSPF,* 67, crsm, 7, pp. 210–11

Roudil, J. L., 1966, L'aménagement des habitats en grotte au Chalco-lithique. *BSPF,* 63, pp. 513–21

Roudil, J. L., 1972, Les techniques décoratives de la céramique pré-historique du Languedoc Oriental. *BSPF,* 69, pp. 430–43

Roudil, J. L., 1973, Le Néolithique d'Italie du Sud et ses affinités avec le Chasséen méridional *BSPF,* 70, crsm, 4, pp. 108–111

Roudil, J. L., Bazile, F. and Soulier, M., 1969, L'habitat campaniforme de Saint-Côme et Maruéjols (Gard). *BSPF,* 66, crsm, 3, pp. 88–91

Roudil, J. L. and Saumade, H., 1968, La grotte de Peyroche II à Auriolles (Ardèche). *Gallia Préhistoire,* 11, pp. 147–203

Roudil, J. L. and Soulier, M., 1969, La grotte du Pont de Maron (Remoulins – Gard) et les bracelets cylindriques en calcaire. *BSPF,* 66, crsm, 8, pp. 244–6

Rozoy, G., 1970, Particularités de l'Epipaléolithique (Mésolithique). *BSPF,* 67, crsm, 8, pp. 237–9

Rozoy, G., 1971, Tardenoisien et Sauveterrien. *BSPF,* 68, pp. 345–74

Sacchi, D., 1971, Recherches sur le Paléolithique et le Mésolithique en

Languedoc Occidental. Campagne de Fouilles 1971. *Cahiers Ligures,* 20, pp. 157–68

Salles, J., 1970, Le dolmen de Peyro Blanco à St Julien-de-Valgalgues (cne. de St Julien-les-Rosiers, Gard). *BSPF,* 67, crsm, 2, pp. 51–5

San Valero, J., 1950, *La Cueva de la Sarsa.* Servicio de Investigacion Prehistorica, Valencia. Trabajos Varios 12

Sangmeister, E. and Schubart, M., 1972, Zambujal. *Antiquity,* 46, pp. 191–7

Savory, H. N., 1968, *Spain and Portugal.* Thames and Hudson, London

Schmid, E., 1960, Über eine Ausgrabung im Bereich der Silex-Bergwerke von Veaux bei Malaucène (Vaucluse). *Der Anschnitt,* 12 (6), pp. 3–11. Bochum

Schmid, E., 1963, Vom Silex-Bergbau bei Veaux-Malaucène in Süd-frankreich. *Der Anschnitt,* 15 (3), pp. 10–21

Schubart, H. and Pascual, V., 1964, Datación por el Carbono 14 de los estratos con cerámica cardial de la Coveta de l'Or. *Archivo de Prehistoria Levantina,* 11, pp. 45–51

Shotton, F. W., Blundell, D. J. and Williams, R. E. G., 1970, Birming-ham University Radiocarbon Dates IV. *Radiocarbon,* 12, pp. 385–99

Simonnet, G., 1971, Informations archéologiques. Circonscription des Antiquités Préhistoriques Midi-Pyrénéees. *Gallia Préhistoire,* 14, pp. 393–420

Siret, E. and Siret, L., [not dated] *Las Primeras Edades del Metal en el Sudeste de España* (excs. 1881–7).

Smith, C. D., 1972, Late Neolithic Settlement, Land-Use and *Garigue* in the Montpellier region, France. *Man,* 7, pp. 397–407

Smith, M., 1952, The Mesolithic in the South of France: a critical analysis. *Proc. Prehist. Soc.,* 18, pp. 103–20

Soler García, N., [not dated] *El poblado de la Casa de Lara, Villena* (*Sep. 1955*)

Souville, G., 1972, La céramique cardiale dans le Nord de l'Afrique, *in Die Anfänge des Neolithikums vom Orient bis Nordeuropa* (ed H. Schwa-bedissen) 7, pp. 60–71

Stevenson, R. B. K., 1947, The neolithic cultures of south-east Italy. *Proc. Prehist. Soc.,* 13, pp. 85–100

Switsur, V. R., 1973, The radiocarbon calendar recalibrated *Antiquity,* 47, pp. 131–7

Tarradell, M., 1962, *El país valenciano del Neolítico a la Iberazación.* Universidad de Valencia, Facultad de Filosofía y Letras, Laboratorio de Arqueología

Taschini, M., 1964, Il livello mesolitico del Riparo Blanc al Monte Circeo. *Boll. Paletnol. Ital.,* 73, ns, 15, pp. 65–88

Taschini, M., 1968, La datation au C14 de l'abri Blanc (Mont Circe). Quelques observations sur le mésolithique en Italie. *Quaternaria,* 10, pp. 137–65

Tine, S., 1970, Notiziario. *Riv. Sci. Preist.*, 25, pp. 427–8

Tine, S., 1971, Notiziario. *Riv. Sci. Preist.*, 26, pp. 488–9

Tixier, J., 1963, *Typologie de l'Epipaléolithique du Magreb*

Tozzi, C., 1966, Il giacimento mesolitico di Capo d'Acqua (L'Aquila). *Boll. Paletnol. Ital.*, ns, 17, pp. 13–25

Treinen, F., 1970, Les poteries companiformes en France. *Gallia Préhistoire*, 13, pp. 53–107

⚹ Trump, D., 1966, *Central and Southern Italy before Rome*. Thames and Hudson, London

Vernet, J.L., 1971, Analyse de Charbons de Bois des Niveaux Boréal et Atlantique de l'Abri de Châteauneuf-les-Martigues (Bouches-du-Rhône). *Bulletin du Muséum d'Histoire Naturelle de Marseille*, 31, pp. 97–103

Vicent, A.M. and Muñoz, A.M., 1973, Segunda Campaña de Excavaciones. La Cueva de Los Murciélagos, Zuheros (Córdoba) 1969. *Excavaciones Arqueológicas en España*, 77

Villalta, Dr, 1971, Las Cuevas del Toll. *Tele/expres* 12 August 1971, Moya, pp. 36–37

Vita-Finzi, C., 1969, *The Mediterranean Valleys*. Cambridge University Press

Vogel, J. C. and Waterbolk, H. T., 1967, Groningen Radiocarbon Dates III. *Radiocarbon, 9*, pp. 107–55

Wainwright, G., 1970, Mount Pleasant. *Current Archaeology*, 23, pp. 320–3

Walker, D. S., 1960, *The Mediterranean Lands*. Methuen, London

Walker, M., 1972, Cave dwellers and cave artists of the neothermal period in South-east Spain. *Transactions of Cave Research Group of Gt. Britain*, 14, No. 1, pp. 1–22

Whitehouse, R. D., 1968a, Settlement and Economy in Southern Italy in the Neothermal Period. *Proc. Prehist. Soc.*, 34, pp. 332–67

Whitehouse, R. D., 1968b, The early neolithic of Southern Italy. *Antiquity*, 42, pp. 188–93

⚹ Whitehouse, R. D., 1969, The Neolithic Pottery of Southern Italy. *Proc. Prehist. Soc.*, 35, pp. 267–310   *pg 298*

Whitehouse, R. D., 1971, The last hunter-gatherers in Southern Italy *World Archaeology*, 2, pp. 239–52

⚹ Whitehouse, R. D., 1972, The rock-cut tombs of the central Mediterranean. *Antiquity*, 46, pp. 275–81   *pg 272*

Whittle, E. H., 1973, Dating of pottery from Neolithic/Chalcolithic sites in Portugal. (Paper delivered at Oxford Symposium on Archaeometry and Archaeological Prospection).

Yengoyan, A., 1968, Demographic and Ecological Influences on Aboriginal Australian Marriage Sections *in Man the Hunter* (ed R. Lee and I. Devore), pp. 185–99

# Index

Names of sites are in **bold type**
References to maps are in **bold figures**
References to illustrations in *italics*